AF255455

Table of Contents

Introduction

Love is the most powerful force in the world. It has the power to create, destroy, heal and make us whole. It is a many splendored thing that makes the world go round. Yet there are those of us human beings who find it very difficult to love ourselves unconditionally.

Self-love is a concept that has been around for many years, but it's only recently been receiving attention as an actual topic among experts in psychology and the like. Many people are familiar with the idea of loving oneself, or being self-confident. But in reality, what does self-love look like? The term is not as popular as some might think, but it's still very important to your life. Self-love is about avoiding being so focused on what you don't have that you forget what you do have.

Self-love is about taking care of yourself through good food, good sleep, and being kind to yourself. It's even possible to forgive yourself for mistakes in your past and move forward with a greater appreciation for life. In the end, self-love is the core belief that you deserve the best life has to offer and that self-care doesn't always take too much effort. Most important of all, self-love isn't just reserved for bad days. Self-love is about happiness, and it's sustainable once you experience it.

The idea of self-love is also closely intertwined with taking care of yourself mentally and physically. Too often, people choose to ignore their mental health in favor of being more concerned with their physical health. However, your mental health can also impact your physical health, making self-love even more important in that context.

Having a positive outlook on life can produce one amazing result after another. The idea that you are enough is such an important lesson to learn as you grow up, and if you don't have a strong sense of self-love already, it's never too late to start developing it now.

So, how can you actually achieve self-love? Well, you can start by being kind to yourself. No one is perfect, and it's important to realize this. Don't punish yourself by seeing things in a negative light. If you're not happy with what you're doing right now, why not move on to something that will make you happier? You don't have to settle for something that makes you unhappy.

Instead of pushing yourself too hard every day with all the activities you have planned, take a step back and ask yourself if it's really worth the time. The next time a situation crops up where motivation is lacking, reevaluate if there is some way that your dedication could be improved.

Self-love is about being true to yourself. Don't allow others to force you into situations that make you feel uncomfortable or even unsafe. If this means cutting off a negative relationship, then so be it. You don't have to worry about what others think of you if you know your feelings are genuine and not based on what other people expect.

It's also important that self-love isn't used as a shield against the real world. While it's healthy to have a positive outlook on life, don't shut out the negatives altogether because that can leave you unprepared for some difficult situations in life. Self-love can be a great motivator for when it's needed the most. If you're struggling with a difficult decision, thinking about what you need and the way you feel about yourself can help quite a bit.

And of course, don't forget that self-love is about being kind to others too. This doesn't mean that you have to love everyone in your life all the time, but it does mean that if someone has done something good for you, acknowledge and thank them. This kind of appreciation goes two ways. It not only makes the other person feel good inside, but it also helps bring positivity into your own life as well.

With this in mind, what can you do to begin practicing self-love? One great way to start is by learning how to meditate. Meditation is a practice of self-awareness that allows you to recognize the chinks in your armor and help you work on them. Even if some parts of your life aren't working out quite as well as others, it's okay. You won't be punished for not being perfect every single day. It's also important to start treating yourself better, from the inside out. This means eating healthy foods and getting enough sleep. It also means being kind to yourself and not allowing anyone else to make you feel bad.

Self-love can be a tough nut to crack, but once you have it, the rewards are endless. Self-love isn't just a goal in itself; it's a journey that will always lead you in the right direction. It's about knowing that every single moment in your life is precious and that you deserve the best life has to offer each and every day.

So what does self-love mean to you? Well, that depends on your own interpretation. If you feel like you need a reminder of what self-love is all about, read on. If you don't know what it means to love yourself already, this book is for you. Self-love doesn't just start when something bad happens. It's something that gets better as time goes by.

Whatever your interpretation of self-love, it's important that you don't ignore it any longer. Instead, learn how to improve every aspect of your life so you can achieve the state of self-love and happiness that will make each day more meaningful. Self-love doesn't happen overnight; it takes time and dedication. But the rewards are worth it, so don't be afraid to make that journey towards self-love. You won't regret it.

The Meaning of Self-Love

What is self-love? It's a state of understanding. It's knowing that everything happens for a reason, and, more importantly, giving yourself the credit you deserve because you have done so much for yourself already, despite what other people think about you or your situation (whether that be good or bad).

Self-love is an attitude. Self-love is a philosophy. Self-love is a way of life.

If you're having trouble defining what self-love means to you, there are a number of ways to look at love and how they relate to self-love:

- Self-love means realizing your own worth and being the best you can be...and never settling for less.
- Self-love means staying true to yourself, following your heart and doing what makes you happy.
- Self-love means treating yourself with kindness and respect...the way that other people treat you.
- If someone loves themselves the way they are, then it's easier for them to accept someone else for who they are as well.
- If you love yourself, others are more likely to love you too.

Self-love is something that everyone deserves and should have no matter what they look like, where they come from, or how much money they make.

Chapter 1
Love Yourself

What is Self-love?

"I may not have gotten where I am today, but if I tried at all, I wouldn't regret one thing that happened along the way. No one gets very far in life by worrying about what may or may not happen by taking life too seriously and trying to control it. That doesn't make any sense." – Johnny Carson

"If you keep doing what you've always done, you'll get what you've always got."-Unknown author

Love is a choice. We can choose to love ourselves through health and wellness or we can choose to love ourselves by abusing our bodies and starting eating disorders. We can choose to love ourselves through positive self-talk or we can choose to love ourselves by putting ourselves down. We can choose to love ourselves positively or negatively, and it is up to us which path we take.

Self-love is a very important part of who we are as human beings; it isn't something that just happens. It can be worked at, just like anything else in life. The first step to self-love is self-acceptance. Self-acceptance takes time and effort; but it doesn't take anything away from you. It can only add to you. It helps you to love yourself in a positive way, helping to bring out the best in yourself and your life.

There are many different aspects of self-love: physical, emotional, spiritual, mental - and more. It is important for everyone to have some form of self-love as well as love for others around them to gain an understanding of their place in the world and how they fit in with all the other people and things that surround them.

Some people need to work on loving themselves in the physical and mental areas of life; for others, it is important to work on self-acceptance and self-growth so they find happiness and fulfilment. It is as much about the present as it is about the future because self-love creates a desire to be happy and gives you energy. Love also makes you want to achieve your goals in life by making you want to grow. It helps us become happy and healthy and lets us love others unconditionally without holding back. Unconditional love means that we have unconditional respect for ourselves.

People who love themselves in a positive way have a good self-image. They look to the future with hope and positive ideas of what they want; they continually strive for their dreams and goals. People who give up on their dreams and goals stop loving themselves in a positive way. They start creating excuses to put them off because they believe that they are out of their reach or not important. The most important thing in life is to have faith, vision and direction; but without these components we feel lost.

So many people think love is about being pampered and getting everything they want from others. They think that if they are nice to everyone around them they will be loved in the long run, but this just doesn't work. Being loved by yourself is a lot harder than being loved by someone else. It takes a lot of self-love to feel good enough about yourself to make yourself happy and then be able to give that love back to others in a more positive way.

Depression can also stop you from loving yourself, and so you are probably feeling low and angry as well as sad. You are feeling sad about what has happened, what you are going through or have gone through. You are angry because you feel hopeless and help-less. You are feeling low because your self-worth is so low that you don't feel like living anymore. But remember that it is possible to feel good enough about yourself to love yourself and others in a more positive way.

Your thoughts can be the biggest barrier to loving yourself properly, as they can send out the wrong signals to your body, brain and nervous system, which in turn will make you feel de-pressed and unable to love yourself properly. Below I have out-lined some of the most common thoughts that can cause you to experience depression and offer some solutions to reduce them.

Complainers – Complainers are people who constantly complain about life, especially when they don't get what they want. As we know, people like to complain because it is a way of feeling better after experiencing something traumatic or upsetting. It is also a way of making oneself feel more important when in reality we are just jealous of the person who annoys us and/or angry at them for having what we don't have instead of focusing on the present moment. If you are a complainer, first stop it or don't do it to begin with. However, if you have been caught into this habit for a very long time and find it hard to stop, there are some ways you can help yourself.

1. Try to love the person who is making you feel this way. Think about how happy they look when they are a complainer and try to put yourself in their shoes and think about how good that would make them feel. You are basically saying that you would rather be miserable than happy. Maybe it is time to start loving yourself again.

2. Try to understand this person. Who made them like this? What made them this way and how can you change their behaviour towards you? Can it be something that happened in the past or something happening now?

3. Sometimes people who always complain just want attention or love, and if you give it to them, they will get jealous and look for other people who don't care about them and tell them off! This will make them feel bad as well as make you look bad to others.

4. Complainers practice a bad habit that you can fall into and not be aware of it. Try to recall when you were last happy without feeling guilty or ashamed. This will remind you that there is happiness in the present moment and that is what we should all be focusing on.

<u>Comparison</u> – Comparison is one of the most common problems; many people are constantly comparing themselves to others, especially if they look down on them or have jealousy issues or are insecure. This can be a problem for people who feel they are missing out on something, because if they are not happy with what they have, or what others have, they will compare themselves to those people who seem to be more perfect, and this can lead to depression and low self-esteem. People who compare themselves tend to spend a lot of money on things that are unnecessary just because they feel they deserve them, and it takes their happiness away. Think about why you compare yourself so much?

1. Look at how you compare yourself to other people and stop feeling bad in the process. People who are unhappy with themselves will go to others who seem to be better than them and compare

themselves to these people, but they never really compare themselves at all. Instead they spend a lot of time comparing themselves internally which only makes them feel worse about themselves.

2. Don't compare yourself to those in your life who are constantly negative about their lives. Look at the good things you have; try not to forget them and think about all the bad things you don't have.

3. Focus your time on improving yourself. If you feel good about the things that you have done so far, compare yourself to other people who are younger. Look at what they have gained and focus on what you have done instead of feeling bad about the things you don't have yet or haven't accomplished. This will help put a fillip on your self-esteem and make you feel better about yourself without comparing yourself to others.

4. Even if you're not great at sports, dancing, or anything else, don't compare yourself to others who are great. Focus on what you can do well or what makes you happy and then sit back and watch the rest of 'the game" play itself out.

5. Don't compare yourself to others in this world who have more money or more of anything than you do. It is a million miles between where we are and where they are. We should all be happy

with what we have and strive to get even better things in life. In this way we can avoid comparisons with those who have way more than we do! We have a chance to make the world a better place – for ourselves and others – and it can start today. Start small and let it grow.

I hope this chapter has given you an idea of how to get yourself out of the "should" trap. Now think about what you can do that will make your world a better place and do it today!

Chapter 2
Self-Comprehension and Acceptance

Self-acceptance is defined as an awareness of your strengths and weaknesses, and a realistic appraisal of your talents, capabilities, and worth. It is part of self-love. This includes a feeling of satisfaction with yourself despite any flaws you may have (which we all do) and regardless of the mistakes you may have made in the past. Self-acceptance is a key factor in achieving success.

Progress can only begin when you fully accept yourself and your fears - all included. When you accept yourself, you will stop beating yourself up because you will love yourself too much. Accepting who you are completely and wholeheartedly is not something that comes easily or naturally. It is going to take some time to get used to it. Being able to accept your worries and that there are just some things you cannot control no matter how badly you may want to will free up the burden being a worrier has placed on your shoulders. This is the reality: there are just some things you cannot control, and it is time to learn to be okay with that.

Many people put on a mask to hide who they are really. The question is, *are you one of them?* Why do people feel confident this way? Why do they feel the need to hide their true personality?

When you put on the mask that you show the rest of the world, you are pretending to be someone else. When you put on that mask, you are hiding the flaws you do not want to acknowledge, and you hope that nobody will notice them either. Wearing a mask has become such a necessity that without it, you do not feel confident being around other people. Wearing a mask and hiding is a more common occurrence than you think.

People wear a mask to pretend to be someone they are not just to fit into social situations. They want to hide the flaws they do not want to admit they have. Some of these masks might be you or they might be your sister, brother, friend, partner, spouse, teenager, colleague, mom, dad, family member, and more. The mom has it all together. Then there is people pleaser, the macho man, the popular girl, the socialite, and the frat boy. There are so many masks that anyone can wear at any given time. Some people even wear multiple masks depending on the social situation.

If you feel like the social encounters in public require a lot more effort than they should, it is likely you are wearing a mask. You probably never noticed it until now because you did not give it a name. The masks we wear are created to protect ourselves from embracing the fear we feel. Exposing our true personalities can be scary. What if we are rejected? What if everyone hates us? What if we are our worst social fears come to life? So yes, your masks might feel nice. It might feel good to have a shield that protects you from getting hurt. It might feel nice to expose yourself and not feel vulnerable. However, the truth of the matter is, *your mask is holding you back in life.*

We are here on this planet for a reason. We are meant to experience the entire spectrum of human emotion. We are meant to go through the difficulties of life. We are all unique individuals, and the fact that some feel the need to hide their personalities is a real shame. If you continue to hide the person you are meant to be, you are never going to live your life the way it is meant to be lived. Suffering from low self-esteem makes it hard to hold yourself in high regard because you cannot see your own value. All you will be able to focus on are your flaws and how you are not good enough. You will constantly be comparing yourself to others.

You have the right to express yourself in any way you want. No one can or should take that away from you. Sure, maybe not everyone is going to love or agree with you, but that is okay. Reflect on the achievements you have accomplished so far. Think about all the times when you made successful decisions. Focus on your strengths and use the time alone with yourself to reinforce reminders of how much you are capable of when you learn to trust yourself.

It is not a bad thing to love yourself, and no one should make you feel guilty about it. If you are going to constantly rely on others to feel worthy, you will never become the improved version of yourself that you long to be. Self-love is not to be confused with narcissism. That is being in love with yourself, which is a different matter altogether.

Self-love is a reminder that you are good enough the way you are, and you deserve good things to happen to you. If you can tell the people you love how amazing and incredible they are and how deserving they are of love, why not do the same for yourself? For happiness to exist long-term, self-love needs to be present—the *real you*. Be gentle and be kind. Love yourself as unconditionally as you love the people in your life. This will reinforce your confidence and self-esteem. We all make mistakes, but beating yourself up repeatedly over them until you are no longer confident is not the way to go about it either.

Chapter 3
Self-Care

Self-care as a dimension of self-love can be vital in reducing stress and anxiety, which in turn will encourage you to be more proactive. It will help you combat disease. It can change how people regard you and how you look at yourself, diminishing negative perceptions. It is not an understatement to say that achieving rounded, responsive self-care is an essential goal in your journey toward self-love.

Let us take a proper look at some of the methods that can guarantee you are getting the self-care you need. Never forget that practice makes perfect, so if any of these suggestions I am about to give you do not give you the results you are hoping for, then you must make a promise to yourself not to give up. Do not underestimate the importance of sustaining good self-care. This is not a one-time solution, and this must be a way of being for the rest of your life. So, let me take you through my six-point self-care plan:

You need the right vitamins, minerals, and proteins to sustain you through the mental and physical demands of daily life. If you lack energy, you will soon become listless and unmotivated. You will also find you have a reduced ability to remember things. Fatigue inevitably leads to negativity. Eating poorly increases the threat of adding extra unhealthy weight. In addition, of course, the risk of heart disease, diabetes, and joint pain is greater. By eating poorly I mean consuming too much sugar, fats, and processed meats, having too few fresh vegetables, berries, and fish, without balance and variety. Why undermine your efforts to love yourself by pursuing an unhealthy diet? Why shorten your life when you are taking the right steps to make it better?

I also want you to give yourself time to digest your food. For centuries, if not millennia, Chinese medicine has talked up the connection between gut health and mental wellbeing. Bacteria in the stomach lining can affect mood and behavior. If you are rushing a meal or eating while standing up, you are doing untold gut damage. All of us like to save time by snacking on the move or completing other activities over food. (I am talking about watching TV or typing up that urgent report.) However, we should avoid this at all costs. It must stop. Allow yourself to sit and calmly finish your meal, remembering to chew each mouthful properly!

That does not mean you cannot treat yourself every now and then. Sometimes it is hugely beneficial to kick back, with your feet up, and watch a good movie or to take a warm bath. How about having a massage, going to a music event, or visiting an art gallery? Hold on to those simple but powerful pleasures. Speaking of which, remember to embrace the happy times of your childhood too, the tastes and activities that gave you so much delight when you were younger. That is a good way to treat yourself! Recapturing those experiences really helps you to channel a more innocent age of youth.

Have a think now about them—whether it be embracing the creativity of a child through drawing or making something with your hands (cookies, a model airplane) or eating your favorite ice cream—and access these moments of joy whenever you are seeking a comforting boost. In addition, yes, I know I said not too much sugar or indulgences, but a little treat from time to time is a boost for your spirit. Believe me, your inner you will certainly thank you for it, as long as you keep as your motto, nothing in excess, everything in moderation.

This all contributes to learning how to relax fruitfully. I am not talking about surfing social media, which often just creates more anxiety, negative thoughts, and feelings of inadequacy. Not all of us can keep up with the Kardashians! What I mean when I say, relaxing is enjoying activities such as walking the dog. Having a lovable pet to care for can be an ideal way to reduce stress and open a mind that is feeling closed, as well as provide a companion. Reading a good book a bit like this one! can also be hugely rewarding. It can keep you free from the clamor of Instagram or Facebook. Get lost in other worlds and ideas; take a break from your worries. I promise you will feel the benefits before too long.

What I am saying to you is step back and slow down. Free from distractions and anxieties, you can focus on all that is good around and within you. Only then will you find tranquility. How about taking a break from your usual routine by going away for a night or weekend? To coin an old phrase, a change is as good as a rest. If you are unable to afford the time or expense of a trip, try walking at lunchtime or at the end of a busy day. Relish all that is glorious about your surroundings and maximize the joys of being outdoors.

Set aside some moments in your weekly routine when you can be active. Keeping fit—vital to maintaining a healthy heart in so many ways and on a number of levels—need not just be about lengthy spells at the gym, pumping iron. Ensure you allow yourself the space within your agenda to do something like swimming or trying out the tango! The key to finding and nurturing that me-time is a simple maxim: never stretch yourself too thin by taking on too much. That is a central part of stepping back; trust me on that. Perhaps find ways of reducing your workload or managing your time better.

Lists are a tried and tested part of achieving better time management. They are an important way to focus the mind and restore a sense of order in what might otherwise seem a chaotic world. Plans, schedules, and agendas can all help dispel a sense of being out of your depth, unsure of what to concentrate on next. They can also make it easier to see where your priorities should be on a day-to-day basis. Reducing the muddle and stress within your head can only be a good thing. There is nothing wrong with writing down what you need to do and setting goals, as long as you don't nag yourself for not always completing them fully. Yes, be disciplined. However, this exercise is about freeing yourself, not creating more walls and less breathing space. Why not also use list-making as an opportunity to write down all that you appreciate, everything that has gone right in your day and all that you have achieved, however seemingly minor? Being reminded of everything you have accomplished and all that is good in your world is a key part of maintaining a positive sense of wellbeing. So, make a note of everything you take pleasure in and are thankful for, along with what you are fortunate enough to have from hot water or a roof above your head to friends and family.

I mentioned the importance of rest. A lack of sleep can cause real mental health problems. It creates a vicious circle of ongoing exhaustion and depression. There is no shame in taking an early night once in a while to catch up on vital shut-eye. Of course, establishing a regular sleeping schedule is important, but if you find yourself tired, go to bed. Ensure, too, that the room you sleep in is a perfect comfort zone. Get it just how you want it to be. This needs to be your go-to place when you feel as if everything is getting on top of you.

On that note, do not be afraid to ask for help. If everything just feels too much, seek the advice of a therapist or a coach. Books like this one are also beneficial to the process. I am truly glad you have thought to reach out and seek the guidance I can offer.

Chapter 4
Self-Respect

Gratitude is being thankful and acknowledging or appreciating whatever is good in your life or any kindness someone shows you. You may not realize it, but gratitude has immense power. It can potentially change your life for the better. An act of gratitude can help you apologize, solve conflicts, and make amends in your relationships. Being grateful will be intrinsically rewarding for you in the long run. It will enhance your self-love.

When you realize that not all that you have is guaranteed for tomorrow, your sense of gratitude will automatically be stronger. So, stop taking your partner and your happy relationship for granted. The law of attraction will pull better into your relationship when you show that you appreciate what you already have.

Benefits of Gratitude

- Improvement in physical, mental, and spiritual wellbeing
- Improvement in social relationships
- Greater feelings and thoughts of happiness and increased optimism
- Increased connection with others in times of loss or any crisis
- Higher levels of energy

- ♥ Improved emotional intelligence
- ♥ Decreased blood pressure
- ♥ Healthier cardiovascular system
- ♥ Higher capacity to forgive others
- ♥ Decreased level of stress, anxiety, or depression
- ♥ Improvement in efforts for self-care
- ♥ Increased sense of spirituality
- ♥ Higher likelihood to lead a healthier lifestyle

Impact of Gratitude on Your Relationship

In terms of marriage or relationships, gratitude plays an important role. Gratefulness will help you take notice of all that is good in your relationship. A lot of people tend to stop looking at the good in their partners and start focusing on the bad at some point. It is great fun at the beginning of the relationship, but things tend to go south from there. You will be more inclined to notice what your partner does not do for you or lacks instead of focusing on all they do and have done for you. People fail to notice that giving and taking goes both ways. Your partner might make less of an effort in your relationship if you do not make much either.

Expectations increase, but actions take a back seat. Everyone is waiting for the other to do more and prove their worth. However, what if you retrain your mind and start over. Why don't you start paying attention to the little things that your partner has always been doing for you? These little things are often more significant than the grand gestures. They might not bring you flowers as often, but they still do the dishes at night for you. Your partner might not get all dressed up every time you go out now, but they always make sure your laundry is done. Things would be so much better in your relationship if you started thinking about the good instead of the bad. In addition, it is not just about thinking. It is important to express gratitude. Appreciation gives validation to their efforts.

When you stop thanking them or showing some form of appreciation, they will lack the will to do much for you. Gratitude will do so much for you personally and your relationship. It will instill happiness and positivity in your partner. They will appreciate the fact that you take the time to express your appreciation of their actions.

You have to create this kind of positive cycle in your relationship, not one where both keep blaming each other for what the other does not do or how little they care. All the complaining and cribbing will only make things go downhill in your relationship. However, using words and actions to show that you are grateful will make a lot of difference.

Gratefulness needs to be cultivated in your mind so that it becomes the natural way you always think. It will help you see what is going right in your life even when other things could go wrong. The law of attraction allows better things to come your way when you focus on what is good. If you stop taking note of the good things and focus on the bad, you will attract more negativity. Expressing gratitude to the universe for all you have will push more blessings your way.

So start cultivating the habit of gratitude. Show that you appreciate a good weather day, a day off, a good meal, a fun date with your partner, or anything that makes you smile or makes your life easier. No matter how hard your life may seem at times, remember that some people have it much tougher. Think of the good that has happened and thank the universe for it. Believe that you will be blessed with more.

Ways to Cultivate Gratitude

The following tips will help you cultivate gratitude every single day in your life.

Keep a gratitude journal. Adding this one positive exercise to your everyday routine will barely take any time, but the benefit will increase in multiples over time. A gratitude journal allows you to keep a record of all the things and experiences you are grateful for in your life. Take a few minutes and write down at least three positive things from a particular day. You can appreciate and be grateful for the bigger blessings in your life, but this journaling will allow you to take notice of the smaller ones as well. For instance, you can be grateful for a day with cool winds during a hot summer. You might be grateful for the nice meal you had or even something like a good conversation you shared with a friend. When you record such positive things, it will help you create a habit of thinking positively. You will be more alert and appreciative of all the good things that happen every day.

Most people these days choose to notice only what goes wrong and focus on that. This cultivates negativity. You can counter this behavior and cultivate gratitude and positivity in your life. The gratitude journal will help you be more enthusiastic about your days and more determined to make the next day a good one as well. You might face challenges, and something bad might happen on some days. However, you can choose to focus on the things that went right instead. People who practice gratitude journaling tend to be happier and more positive.

Focus on gratitude for a few minutes at the end of every day. Take some deep breaths and think of the things you are grateful for. Thank the higher powers for your blessings and your ability to overcome any challenges that come your way. Be mindful and present as you do this gratitude exercise. Think of all the good things that have happened to you throughout your day. If some person helped make your day better, write a thank-you note and pass it on the next day. Tell them that you are thankful that they helped in making your day good. Expressing gratitude will make them appreciate this gesture and feel appreciated. If your partner made you a good meal or just took time to ask about your day, thank them for it. Show them that you are grateful for their efforts and their presence in your life.

Avoid complaining as much as possible. When you constantly crib or complain about something, you are focused on the negativity of the day. Instead, choose to let it go. If you can improve something, spend your energy on working on it instead of complaining. If you have no control over it, avoid obsessing over it.

Every morning when you wake up, take some time to express gratitude. Think of the things you are grateful for and what you hope for the day as well. Repeat some positive affirmations and watch them unfold into reality.

Gratitude meditation is another way to build positivity. It is a way to train your mind to be more positive, grateful, and happy. Spending a few minutes meditating every day will benefit you a lot in the long term. Find a comfortable place to be seated and relax. Close your mind and take a few abdominal breaths slowly and steadily. Try to feel more grounded where you are seated. When you feel more relaxed, ask yourself what you are grateful for. Think about any one of those things and ponder on it. Absorb the positivity from that grateful incident or thought. Continue to another experience you are grateful for. Try to visualize all this happening once again in your mind. This is how you create a positive chain of thought. It is important to continually remind yourself of your positive experiences because humans tend to hold on to negative experiences more often. Break that chain and let go of the negativity.

Chapter 5
Self-Trust & Self Esteem

A healthy self-esteem is something that happens when a person values himself or herself who they are and enjoys a degree of self-love. The idea of healthy self-esteem comes with the idea that you are a worthy being and have some kind of role to play in how this universe works. Healthy self-esteem includes realizing that humans are fallible and have different characteristics.

Humans make mistakes; in fact, making mistakes is what makes you human. Everyone makes mistakes, and you make certain mistakes in your life. A person with healthy self-esteem happens to be their own best friend, which is why they realize that making mistakes does not necessarily make them a bad person. It just makes them human.

People with low self-esteem see making mistakes as a sign of their uselessness. Every single mistake they make is followed by sessions of over-thinking where they dissect the mistake and hate themselves further for erring in judgment. The end conclusion after these hours of thinking is that they happen to be useless and bad for making that small mistake.

A person with healthy self-esteem realizes that making mistakes is not a crime. In addition, they realize how important it is for them to be their own best friend. Befriending yourself is part of healthy self-esteem. When you befriend yourself, you realize that you can err. You can make errors. In addition, when you realize that you can make errors, you realize how to love yourself in spite of them. A person with healthy self-esteem has high self-regard and self-respect, just as you would have for a friend, only that regard and love are now used for oneself.

People with high self-esteem do not like degrading themselves when talking to someone else. They realize that the conversation is temporary and their love and friendship will continue. People who do not have healthy self-esteem degrade and tell jokes about themselves and their bodies. These jokes end up ruining their self-confidence in the end.

Self-esteem is an important part of our life based on how much it affects us. Self-esteem is the filter through which we react to everything we are experiencing and everything that happens to us. You can allow your low self-esteem get to your mind or you can work to improve it for your future success. Remember that the first prerequisite of building healthy self-esteem is to love and befriend yourself.

Why is Self-Esteem Important?

While we have listed different definitions of self-esteem and the healthy aspects of good self-esteem, it is now time to shed some light on the importance of self-esteem.

By now, you must be wondering about the importance of self-esteem in the context of your life. Having high self-esteem is increasingly important because of its benefits in saving you from the downsides of low self-esteem. People with low self-esteem have numerous mental and physical repercussions. They can develop mental illnesses such as anxiety and depression. Problems usually start when a person does not value themselves and what they add to this world.

You are the best version of yourself, and nobody else can top that. The sooner you realize this, the better it is for you. People who have a hard time appreciating themselves for who they are and what they do live within a bubble of low self-esteem. The issues begin when you first start questioning something natural. It could be your height, your physical characteristics, or your voice. You start dreaming and hope you can rid yourself of that characteristic.

That is when you enter the point of no return and start delving into the subjugated world of dreaming. Positive self-esteem, on the other side, includes accepting yourself for what you bring to the table and you do not want it to be any different. Once you start undervaluing yourself, you start seeing a fall in the performance you would want to give. A wide range of problems takes birth when you start undervaluing yourself. These problems include negative thinking, disordered eating habits, abuse, unhealthy relationship pattern, poor body image, underachievement in professional or academic life, and impaired communication skills.

The image you have of yourself is what can save you from falling deep into the pits of depression. Consider self-esteem as the roots of the tree of life. Your roots define how hard or balanced you stand in your life. If your roots are based on a weakened and flawed sense of self, then you will never grow to the limits you have in mind. Stunted mental growth is also a result of low self-esteem where you never achieve the kind of mental growth you want. When you base your life on positive self-esteem, you make sure that your roots remain firm and resilient. While low self-esteem can fluster and shaken you, high self-esteem can save you from complete annihilation or failure in life.

Chapter 6
Self-Talk

S elf-talk is the inner discussion you have with yourself. Everybody engages in self-talk. However, the impact of self-talk is only evident when you are using it positively to enhance self-love. The power of self-talk can lead to an overall boost in your self-esteem and confidence. Moreover, if you convince your inner-self that you are beyond certain emotions, you will also find it easy to overcome emotions that seem to weigh you down.

You cannot be sure that you will always talk to yourself positively. Therefore, it is important to understand that self-talk goes in both directions. At times, you will find yourself reflecting on negative things. In other cases, you will think about the good things you have achieved. This can be understood as pushing yourself to think positively even when you are going through challenges. When you do this, you will approach life more optimistically—as such, overcoming challenges will not be a daunting feat since you can see past the hurdles.

If you are self-talk is always inclined to be negative, it does not mean there is nothing you can do about it. With regular practice, you can shift your negative thinking into positive thinking. In time, this will transform you into a more optimistic person who is full of life.

Importance of Positive Self-Talk

Research shows that positive self-talk can have a positive impact on your general wellbeing. The following are among the goals you strive for by regularly practicing positive self-talk.

Boost Your Confidence

Maybe you do not completely believe in your skills and abilities. Well, positive self-talk can transform the perceptions you have about yourself and your abilities. Unfortunately, we overthink the things we feel we should do. Therefore, instead of acting, you end up wasting your time overthinking about them. Positive self-talk lets you put aside any doubts about accomplishing a particular goal. Therefore, you will be motivated to act without worrying whether you will succeed or not. You become optimistic about life. There is nothing that can stop you from trying your best.

Save Yourself from Depression

Overthinking can make you susceptible to depression because you garner the perception that you are incapable of performing well. This affects your emotional and physical wellbeing. Some of the effects you will experience when you are depressed include a lack of sleep, lethargy, loss of appetite, nervousness, etc. Positive self-talk can change all this. It will fill you with the optimism you need to see past your challenges. As a result, instead of believing you cannot do something, you convince yourself that you can. Positive self-talk can transform how you feel; it is just a matter of changing how you perceive the world around you.

Eliminate Stress

There are many stressors to overcome every day. We all go through stress; the only difference is how we deal with it. Some people allow stress to overwhelm them. Often, you find folks with a negative outlook on life. They will have all sorts of negative comments like "Life is hard," "I can't take it anymore," "I'm always tired," "Things never get easier," etc. We have heard such comments coming from our friends who have given up on life.

The reality is that stress can get the best of you if you surrender. Practicing positive self-talk can help you realize that stress comes and goes. As it is common thing that everybody experiences, there is no need to allow it to overwhelm you. When you begin to understand that you can change how you think to overcome stress, you will be less anxious. As such, this reduces the likelihood of overthinking.

Protect Your Heart

We all know that stress is not good for our health. Stress leads to many diseases, including cardiovascular diseases such as stroke.

Therefore, by practicing positive self-talk, you will be protecting your heart.

Boost Your Performance

Positive self-talk can also boost your performance in anything you do. It affects how you attend to your daily activities. With positive self-talk, you can tap into your energy reserves and boost your performance. It is surprising how quickly you change how you feel by thinking positively.

How Positive Self-Talk Works

Before getting into detail about practicing self-talk, it is important to understand how negative thinking works. There are several ways to think negatively, including:

- ♥ **Personalizing:** This form of negative thinking occurs when you blame yourself for anything bad that happens to you.

- ♥ **Catastrophizing :** If you expect the worst to happen to you, then you are simply catastrophizing everything. The issue here is that you do not allow logic to help you understand that some things are not the way you think.

- ♥ **Magnifying:** Here, you pay more attention to negative things. In most cases, you block your mind from thinking positively about any situation you might be going through.

- ♥ **Polarizing:** You look to extremes when it comes to judging wat is happening around you. From the perceptions you have developed in your mind, something is either good or bad.

The importance of identifying these forms of negative thinking is that you can transform them into positive thinking. Sure, on paper, this might sound like an easy task. However, the truth is that it takes time to live an optimistic life. You need to practice positive self-talk every day and in everything you do.

Chapter 7
Setting Goals

Goal setting is a key to productivity. It is the process of figuring out the outcomes you want in life in general so you have a solid framework to work off and you actually make progress. There is nothing like progress to boost one's self-love. Many people are like driftwood, floating and going nowhere exactly, even if on the surface you can see they are working hard to make something of themselves. For the most part, they have no set destination. Does this sound like you? Well, if it does, we are going to fix that by setting some goals the right way. When you have properly set your goals, you will find yourself being naturally productive.

Goal Setting and Productivity

The 80/20 rule or Pareto Principle states that there are a natural division of people in society into two distinct groups when it comes to how much influence and money they have:

- The Trivial Many. Alternatively, the bottom 80 percent.
- The Vital Few. Alternatively, the top 20 percent.

All things in the economy are subject to this same principle, where 80 percent of the country's wealth is actually controlled by 20 percent of the population. You can apply this same 80/20 rule to almost anything in life, including goal setting and productivity.

In applying the Pareto Principle to goal setting, 80 percent of your results are determined by 20 percent of your activities. In other words, if you have a list of 10 super urgent, important things to get to, then only 2 out of those 10 things will be worth more than the remaining 8 together. It is a very sad state of affairs that, for the most part, people will place more importance on the trivial 8 rather than the vital 2, which would give them the success and productivity they seek.

If you want to apply the 80/20 rule to productivity and goal setting in your life, then you have to do a few things:

1. Write down 10 goals. Once you are done, it is time to get real with yourself. Ask yourself, if there was only one thing you could make happen on that list, right here and now, which one would it be? This is how you get successful. Ask yourself what the second most important goal is. Keep going with the questions as you run through your list.

2. Work on your chosen goals all the time. Remember, it is not about being busy. Productivity is not about being all over the place, forever swamped, yet accomplishing little to nothing. Save yourself the heartbreak by working on tasks of high value and not procrastinating by taking on unimportant tasks. The tasks that bring you the most value are often the most complex, hardest things. That said, when you are done, the reward is worth it and could completely turn your life around for the better. Before you

get to work each day, figure out the tasks in the 80 percent realm of "not vital" and the ones in the 20 percent realm of "vital." Then pay attention only to the vital 20 percent of your tasks.

3. Forget about dealing with the little things first. Little things are not worth it, and you will never be done with them because they pop up ten times a second! In the end, you will have nothing to show for all your exhaustion when you focus on the little things instead of the big stuff.

Sure, it is tempting to start simple, but do not do that. Always get the hard stuff out of the way first. Make that your brand-new habit, so you can continue to make progress. A recent study was carried out on goal setting to investigate the difference in how poor and rich people go about setting goals. The findings were interesting. One thing they noticed is that 85 percent of the rich have one huge goal they are always working on. Meanwhile, only 3 percent of poor people have a huge goal; it is just that they never work on it much!

You obviously want to be productive. You want wealth. You want success. To get it, you must act as the wealthy do. Success and failure both leave clues behind. Look and study successful people and emulate their behavior. Pick one big thing and keep working on it. This is how you can change your life. Keep in mind that when you have very clear goals, you will always have the perfect answer to make them happen when you need it. This is advice from the one and only Brian Tracy, so you know he knows what he's talking about.

Proven Tricks and Strategies for Goal Setting

One of the people who comes to mind when I think about success and productivity is the great Tony Robbins. That is a man who knows how to set goals and smashes them, and he's a great role model. Let us get into the strategies he suggests for making sure you achieve your goals all the time.

1. The pursuit is just as important as the prize. Many people do not think about the other stuff that happens when trying to make their goals real. A journey will change you forever in one way or another. When you work on your goals, you will change. However, to paraphrase Tony Robbins, the goal of a goal is not about getting it, but about the person you become in the process. This growth is where the real success lies. This growth will show you that you are capable of so much more than you think you could achieve.

2. Have the right timeline in mind. If you set a goal to lose 50 pounds in a month, then unless you are going in for liposuction, let me be the first to heartily announce that you will fail hard and fail big. You need to keep your goals reasonable. If not, you will find yourself constantly disappointed with your lack of progress and overwhelmed by how far you have to go. If your goal will take longer than a year, it helps to set benchmarks by which you can measure your progress so you are inclined to keep going.

3. Focus on the wanted, not the unwanted. If your goal is centered on what you do not want, you are not going to get far. What is it you do want? Do not say to yourself, "I don't want this beer gut." Think, "I want to be lean, fit, strong, and have a healthy BMI." The great Robbins has suggested that whenever you cannot figure out what you want, then you need to **do** something. Take physical action. He suggests going for a run while focusing on what it is you want. When you constantly think about what you do not want versus what you **do** want, you are operating from a fear-based mindset. Change your mindset. I have already shared how you can do that. Become the person who feels the fear and still goes after their goal.

4. Keep going even after you have hit your target. Therefore, you made a million dollars. Congratulations! Do not stop there. Always set new targets to reach. This is how you grow. If you do not have a new target, you are quickly going to find yourself wallowing in fulfillment and depression. It will not matter how lofty the goal you hit is. If you are unfulfilled, you have failed in the biggest and worst possible way.

I am not suggesting you should not take some time to enjoy the fact that you have nailed your goal. You must celebrate. Just make sure you think about what else you want next, make that your new goal, and keep at it. This is the way to stay satisfied with your achievements in life. It is not the goal you want; it is the growth. This is why you have new ones with each one you check off your list.

5. Don't fret about nailing our goals. I know this one probably confuses you. After all, isn't the reason for setting the goal...the goal? The goal is not the goal. **Growth is the goal.** The reason we keep looking for what to do is that we feel the most alive when making progress. The journey, or the progress, is what matters. That is what life is all about. Growth means many things to many people. Figure out what it means for you and aim for that. Seek growth, and you will become the best version of yourself. But when you do, there is always room to stretch some more. That is the beautiful thing about life.

Chapter 8
Overthinking

Signs You Are an Over thinker

The following are clear indications that you think too much. You might deny it but consider these signs and ask whether these are some of the things you might have done or experienced. Overthinking can tax one's ability to enjoy self-love.

You Overanalyze Everything

If you notice that you overanalyze everything around you, then you are certainly an over-thinker. You may try to find a deeper meaning in all the experiences you go through. When meeting new people, instead of engaging in productive communication, you may focus instead on how other people perceive you. Someone could be giving you a particular look, and you may make several assumptions based on that look. Overthinking consumes you. What you do not realize is that not everything has intrinsic meaning.

You Think Too Much But Don't Act

An over-thinker will be affected by something called analysis paralysis. This is a scenario where you think too much about something, but do not do anything about it. In this case, you spend a lot of time weighing the options you have. At first, you make up your mind on what the best alternative might be. Later, you compare your decision to other possible decisions you could take. You cannot stop thinking about the possibilities and whether or not you have made the right decision. Ultimately, you end up not making a decision. You only find yourself in a vicious circle where you simply think a lot, but there is little that you do. Perhaps the best strategy to prevent yourself from falling into a thinking trap is to try out alternatives. A simple decision to act will make a huge difference.

You Can't Let Go

Often, we make erroneous decisions that could lead us to fail. When this happens, it can be daunting to let go, more so when you reflect on the sacrifices you have made to get to the point where you. For example, you might feel that it is painful to let go after you have invested a lot of money in a certain business. The issue here is that you do not want to fail.

However, it is important to realize that failing to let go only holds you back from trying out something else that could work. It also affects your life since you will repeatedly think about your failures. You need to move on. It is important that you shift your attention to something else instead of beating yourself up over something now out of your control. Convince yourself that there is nothing you can do about what has already happened apart from learning from it.

You Always Want to Know Why

Without a doubt, the notion of asking why can be helpful in solving problems. This probing attitude gets you the answers you might be looking for. Nonetheless, it can also be damaging when you cannot help but always wonder why. Normally, we are accustomed to answering questions from kids. They just love to ask about anything and everything. They will not hesitate to ask you why you do not talk to your neighbor, why children are born, or simply why you love to walk. There is something unique about how children are curious. Overthinkers maintain such an investigative attitude throughout their lives. As adults, there are certain things that only have surface meanings. Therefore, probing too much can only affect how other people see you.

You Analyze People

The way you see other people says a lot about you. In most cases, you get lost thinking too much about how other people behave. You may tend to judge everyone you come across. This one walks in a funny way. That person is not dressed well. You wonder what someone sitting in the park is smiling about. When these thoughts fill your head, you only drain yourself. Spending too much time focusing on other people will only deter you from using your mind productively. Instead of visualizing your goals and your future, you waste energy mulling over little things that add no value to your life.

Regular Insomnia

Do you find it hard to sleep sometimes? You may get worked up over the idea that your brain cannot shut down and stop thinking. Sadly, this can paralyze you since your brain does not get the rest it deserves. Gradually, you will notice a decrease in your productivity. You are unlikely to feel good about yourself since you achieve little. If this is something you have been experiencing, you might be an over-thinker. What can you do about it? First, if you are not active, it is vital that you find a way of keeping yourself busy. In addition, meditation is a great practice that can help you stop overthinking, relax, and focus on the present.

You Always Live in Fear

Are you afraid of what the future has in store for you? Living in fear could drive you to resort to drugs and alcohol to help you drown your sorrows and forget. Unfortunately, this is not the case since drugs and alcohol are merely depressants. They slow down brain functioning. As a result, you tend to believe that they are helping your life.

You are Always Fatigued

Do you always wake up in the morning feeling tired? This could be a result of stress or depression. Instead of living a productive life, you find yourself waking up late, tired, and unmotivated. This happens because you do not give your mind an opportunity to rest. It has been working day and night. In the evening, instead of sleeping, you find yourself awake all night because you are overthinking. Your mind cannot work for 24 hours straight at the same level of functioning: you will only suffer from burnout. You need to give your mind ample time to rest and reboot.

You do not live in the Present

Do you find it difficult to enjoy life? Why do you find it daunting to sit back, relax, and be happy with your friends? The mere fact that you cannot stay in the present implies that you are not focusing on what is happening in the present. Overthinking will blind you from noticing anything good that is currently happening around you.

You often think about the worst that can happen. The issue is that you are trapped in your mind, and there is nothing outside your thoughts that you can constructively think about.

Failure to live in the present denies you the opportunity to improve your relationships with other people. In fact, you will live in fear that they will criticize you. Therefore, you only want to exist in your cocoon. Again, this will lead to stress.

Chapter 9
Healthy Living

There are several keys to leading a healthy, vibrant lifestyle as we get older. Self-love means self-care. Certainly, what we put into our bodies will go a long way in determining what we get out of it. But there are other factors that determine how healthy we are as we age. Exercise, how you sleep, and a positive mental attitude are a few of the ingredients for healthy aging, and quite obviously, they are all intertwined. In fact, all these factors fit together like pieces of a puzzle, and to make the picture complete, all the pieces have to be present.

Consider some things to avoid that prevent us from achieving our healthy aging goals.

1. Diet. We might as well face it, we can't eat like we could when we were younger. As pointed out in the recommended caloric intake, with every year we add, the number of daily calories we are allowed to consume goes down. Even by eating the right foods and doing regular detoxing, our liver and other organs just don't run as efficiently as they did when we were kids. But there is no need to fight it. Just understand that it is part of the aging process and make the necessary adjustments.

2. Exercise. This is so important for everybody, but as you age, it will literally keep you alive longer. Even walking, gardening, or

playing golf is helpful, but if you are able to do higher intensity workouts, those exercises will be even better. They keep the metabolism at a higher level, promote better blood circulation, and produce endorphins that promote a more positive outlook on life. And as we know, if we perceive the world to be a better place, studies have shown that it diminishes the aging process.

3. Have an active social life. Companionship is such a huge part of growing older with a great attitude.

4. A few of the things we must avoid are the use of nicotine and other drugs and chemicals, limiting as much as possible the use of medication, and the overuse of alcohol and caffeine, especially late at night. Hopefully, some of these hazardous habits were never picked up over the years, but now would be the perfect time to kick them if you did.

5. Sleeping better

Exercise has a great deal to do with getting better sleep, and sleeping better means more energy during the day. As we exercise during the day, stress and anxiety will be reduced, giving us a longer and deeper sleep. Studies have shown that people who sleep better have an easier time controlling their weight, which of course, makes it less of a burden to exercise. Getting the sleep you need is critical for so many aspects of your general health. For instance, did you know that people who do not get enough sleep are more likely

- ♥ to be obese and suffer from chronic illnesses like diabetes

- ♥ to have a higher incidence of mental illness, including depression and anxiety
- ♥ to have a high incidence of congestive heart failure and drug-resistant hypertension
- ♥ to have conditions like snoring (or obstructive sleep apnea) that tend to make pre-existing problems with sleep even worse

There is no doubt that sleep is important to general health (and general beauty), but here is where most people often get confused because getting "enough: sleep is not necessarily a function of how many hours you sleep. It is a function of the quality of your sleep, which can be understood in the general concept of sleep hygiene. Indeed, simply getting more hours of sleep will not guarantee you all the benefits of sleep. Sleep is not always an independent factor to your health and beauty, but rather, it is highly integrated with your dietary patterns, your general health, your personal habits, your stress levels, your work life, and your social connections.

If the rest of your life is in disarray, then getting more sleep is not necessarily a good thing, and in fact, hyper somnolence (sleeping for extended periods of time) can be a sign of depression or other mental illness. Likewise, insomnia may also be a sign that other things in your life are stressful and problematic, and it is important to not see the "tail wagging the dog" so to speak, in regards to sleep (or lack of it). See your inability to sleep as a symptom rather than a cause of other issues.

Some basic rules for better sleep are: don't eat a big meal before you go to sleep. Insulin is one of the critical hormones needed has to be controlled to ensure a proper night's sleep. As insulin levels rise, they prevent the body's conversion of L-tryptophan into the sleep hormone, melatonin.

Melatonin is crucial to getting a proper night's sleep, and high insulin levels prevented them from doing their job. High insulin levels also prevent the secretion of the human growth hormone during sleep, and they also prevent you from getting into the deeper, more restful cycles (REM) that you need to really get a good rest. Therefore, it is very important not to eat a big meal before you go to sleep, especially one that is high in sugar, which will invariably raise insulin levels.

All drugs such as alcohol and tobacco are strongly discouraged before you go to sleep, as they will disrupt your sleep cycles. Alcohol, although it makes you sleepy initially also prevents you from getting into deep REM sleep. So do stimulants like nicotine and coffee. They should be avoided whenever possible. Likewise, sleeping pills often prevent you from getting into the deep REM sleep necessary to wake up feeling rested and refreshed.

Watching TV or playing on the computer till late at night can disrupt your sleep as well. The artificial light of screens often prevents the conversion of melatonin in the brain and thus interferes with sleep. This includes all of your reading devices, tablets, and smartphones that use blue light technology to provide background light.

Try to be regular about your sleeping patterns. Even if it is the weekend, don't necessarily sleep in. Maybe you will need to take a nap later on, but at least try to experiment with keeping a regular schedule in regards to falling asleep and waking up and see how you feel.

Use blinds if necessary to help you achieve the darkness to stimulate melatonin production and help you get a good night's sleep. Try drinking a glass of herbal tea. Chamomile is very helpful in this regard, as are many other herbal teas like peppermint and spearmint.

Warm baths are also exceptionally helpful. They can help relax you, and mineral salt baths can be very helpful as magnesium is absorbed transdermally to help with sleep. Magnesium helps push calcium out of the muscles, and as a result, it helps muscles can relax. It is often given to pregnant women before they give birth to help with the contraction in the smooth muscle of the uterus.

In addition, magnesium may also have a natural sedative and calming effect on the brain in a similar manner by preventing neurons from becoming "excited" by molecules like calcium and glutamate, which cause neurons to fire.

Melatonin can be an effective supplement that will help you get a restful night's sleep. It may help more than prescription sleeping pills and even over-the-counter sleeping pills.

Exercise always helps as long as it is not strenuous and causes pain and soreness, which will prevent you from sleeping. Many people find it very difficult to work out close to their bedtime, as it tends to keep them awake. Find out what works for you. Finally, who doesn't want to achieve great-looking skin and one of the ways to do this is by getting not just more sleep but better quality sleep.

Practice all these dimensions of self-care and watch your self-love burgeon.

Chapter 10
Confidence and Self-motivation

How do you perceive yourself? Do you think you are strong? Can you manage anything that happens during the day or weeks ahead? Do you break down when things get a little tough? Do you project your feelings or actions onto others? Do you feel you are hiding your inability? The above questions relate to confidence and how you perceive yourself – constituting your self-love. Some people keep going, doing, and never seem to falter. Others talk down about themselves yet still accomplish plenty. Some individuals will project their feelings, and it is the appearance of being "perfect" that motivates them, while ultimately, they lack confidence.

Before you can begin to gain self-motivation and improve your confidence, you need to understand who you are and why you should be working on these two concepts.

Why Learn to Motivate Yourself

We all have dreams that sprout from self-love. When in depression, we sometimes forget about those dreams and believe we cannot accomplish them. We feel we are spinning our wheels, struggling, and perhaps it is someone else's fault rather than our own. Have you had a struggle such as this? Are you in one now?

Depression is just one effect that may cause a lack of self-motivation and confidence. For other individuals, their childhood path never gave them the desire to be motivated. Perhaps you always had someone to depend on to motivate you to do things, and that has continued into adulthood.

Consider for a moment that path of the woman in the '50s. Many women were brought up with minimal schooling, told they would not need college but rather an etiquette school to learn how to be wives, mothers, and the home support for their working husbands. The idea that some would go to college existed, but most often, ladies colleges offered courses in art or teaching, and not areas like science and engineering. The motivation was always about the husband and family. In the same vein, it also created numerous struggles and unhappy moments.

Motivation for these women was based on their upbringing and what they were told they could or could not achieve. Think about how you would feel if your parents told you college was out of the question and all you could do was go to a trade school, marry, and raise children. How would you react? Perhaps, you have been told this as it does still happen today. You might have the thoughts that you want to change this outlook, you want your kids to have more opportunities, and later in life, you finally decide to do something to make changes.

It is not only your obligation to ensure the female gender is regarded with equality but something you should desire in your heart. We can all have the family, happy marriage, and career we want if we are motivated enough to get it.

If you do not want to feel stuck in the '50s with only a few choices and a path that ends in an unhappy marriage, then you must take control of your life and learn how you can motivate yourself. Yes, upbringing is a part of it. We learn from our parents through their perceptions, lessons, and thoughts, but as a human with free will, we truly have the choice to improve our lives based on our own dreams. It doesn't matter how long it takes us to realize these dreams. What matters is that we are willing to try.

Plenty of things can get in the way, from your upbringing to social perceptions, even your own biases. It is going to take stepping back and viewing your life, what you desire, and who you want to become before you find motivation. It may take all the above to discover "why" you should find self-motivation.

Exercise for the 'Why'

Why are some women more motivated than others? Consider Oprah as an example. She has risen to new heights in stardom, with acting in movies, running her own talk show, her TV channel, starting a magazine, and writing books. What motivated her? Interviews she has done say she wanted to prove that as a woman of African American heritage, it was possible to be successful, to help other women realize their potential, and be an inspiration. She has certainly been all those things.

Why might a woman try to harm her family, even though she is divorced? What would keep motivating her to spend energy on negative and destructive pathways? Money, hate, an inability to genuinely love herself? There are positive and negative reasons one might consider to prompt self-motivation in life. Before going into the exercise, it is helpful to point out the difference between self-motivation for progress and positive feelings and the "negative" reasons you might motivate yourself to do something.

It is time to discover "why" you want to find self-motivation:

- What are your dreams?
- Do your dreams feel achievable?
- How can you choose one dream and make it a reality?
- Are you unhappy with your choices in life?
- What can you do to alleviate the negative feelings and find positive emotions?

You do not have to have answers to every question right now. The idea is to discover who you are and why you have the dreams or goals you keep dwelling on. Dreams serve to build self-love and motivation is a key ingredient. You sought a guide for self-motivation because something was making you unhappy. You are trying to find a new way to approach life and reach the dreams you harbor. The exercise is asking you to take the first step and write the goals down. When you visualize them on paper, they become more real. It is also a way for you to examine the goals in full and decide what is achievable in your current situation and what may need to change.

Often the first step to finding more motivation or any at all is to address why you are unhappy and what you can do to ensure a more positive outlook. It takes time. For now, the "why" of learning self-motivation techniques is the most important? As you move through the guide, you will be given more exercises and information to help you reach your goals.

How important is Motivation

Self-motivation provides us with the ability to protect our interests. Without the psychological process of motivation by which we act, we would not reach our objectives or goals. Using motivation allows us to put away our weaknesses and concentrate on the strengths. Motivation is highly imperative to one's success. It offers:

- ♥ Commitment
- ♥ Personal Drive
- ♥ Optimism
- ♥ Initiative

Commitment comes into play when you have personal or career-related goals. Personal drive is all about the desire to meet goals or even exceed your standards. Optimism helps you assess life without the negatives holding you back. Initiative is the part of the motivation that helps you be ready for any opportunity that might present itself. Those who are self-motivated often have confidence, time management skills, and are super organized.

The intrinsic factors of motivation are usually based on feelings, such as love or the desire to follow through. With "self" motivation being intrinsic, you are more likely to perform an act for the satisfaction it provides versus the extrinsic factors that demand satisfaction from others. You can be motivated in different ways, using both intrinsic and extrinsic concepts. What becomes of a person who is not self-motivated or even motivated is—well—nothing. They do not reach their goals. They spin their wheels in the same dead-end jobs and never reach happiness.

Motivation is important for several reasons:
- ♥ to feel love for yourself and to accept it from others
- ♥ to be happy in your life and the choices you make
- ♥ to lead by example for new generations
- ♥ To attain goals and dreams you have
- ♥ to take the initiative on projects and opportunities
- ♥ to stick with something you start and finish it to the end

Without motivation, nothing would be accomplished. We would not have reached the moon, households would not have personal computers, cars would not be a thing, and the list of inventions can go on. No motivation equals a lack of safety, personal triumph, and health care when you think on a global scale.

You are ready to proceed in your education about how the brain works and the concept of neuroplasticity, which will lead you to an understanding of how you can develop self-motivation no matter your age.

Chapter 11
Personal Development

Personal development is a lifetime cycle through which you can assess your talents, identify your goals, and execute actions to achieve your objectives. It is essential for self-love to sustain itself. It is a system that enhances your skills and behaviors to create trends in your life that contribute to the achievement of goals when combined. Progress in different areas of life, such as community, business, finance, and health, is achieved.

Mental preparation is the first step of every mission. Why and how would you like this to be achieved? Motivation is the force that drives you to stick to a strategy and do what is required. Ask yourself, what is my personal growth? What is my part? This will not only encourage you to develop your personality, but it will also educate you on the way to achieve objectives and shape yourself positively in every aspect of life. If you are serious about personal development, I guarantee that after following the easy instructions, you will not only love this book but you will be surprised at your changing life experiences.

Self-Motivation
Self-motivation is makes things happen. It's a key skill in life and not just a power to carry out tasks and goals. You will give this

capability serious consideration if you are interested in personal growth and an intense degree of self-love.

What incentive is there?

Why would you seek to do something that you believe your talents have gone beyond? Remember what you have done and what you are good at. What are you doing now? What's best for you? What are the attributes you don't have that most others do? Stop reading and think about it for 5 minutes. It's going to give you a reason. There are certain parameters of motivation to look at.

1. Risks & failure: You have to keep in mind that reversals and losses are going to take place as you start to develop a balanced personality. Such mistakes should not discourage you from moving further ahead, and they will serve as a lesson in your errors. Not every decision is perfect. You often struggle because of your limitations, and things are beyond your control due to circumstances. Consider your abilities consciously and assess your control over these failures.

2. Just do it. "There must be a single step on a thousand miles road" — Chinese proverb. Just go for it. Stop thinking about tomorrow. This is the perfect time to begin your behavioral growth. The time is now.

3. Surrounding yourself with good company is the theme of a very famous quote: "A man is related to the business he holds." Very few understand this short phrase's meaning and strength. Encircle yourself with motivators. Seek friends with high ambitions. If

you're in a ditch, you can't see the good things out there. Get out of it, sit down and talk to people about goals and proposals. Don't waste time with losers who lack a lick of motivation.

4. Prepare your future: it's never too early to think of your future and what you want to do. You need to think about yourself first. It should not be discouraging to spend time alone. You need some clarification about what you really want before you take action for a better future for yourself.

Ask yourself questions about what you want and not what other people want for you. Outline the main issues you see in your future. Avoid thinking about the past and concentrate on the present and the future. It will allow you to continue to dream. The past is an obstacle if you want to try to move on. To succeed is to go ahead, grow and allow things to happen, to make things possible.

5. Take a look at your life and find your passion— something that naturally comes to you. Any excitement on your way to success will fuel confidence. Begin to feel proud of what is right for you. Strive to get what you want in life. Confidence and ambition work together to improve your chances of doing what you enjoy most. Confidence in your intuition. You have a natural instinct to work with your passion. Track your progress and see how far you vary (as you most certainly will) from your original plan - but don't be afraid.

6. Start small: it takes serious effort to get where you want to go. You need to take small steps to get there. It'll be easy to keep moving forward once you have begun the journey. Perhaps in one day, you can't achieve your ambition. Time, patience, and coherence are required. Take your time. Take some steps to your goal every day, and you'll notice how drastic your life changes will be. It'll be your habit soon, and you'll feel normal once you are committed. Make time every day and focus on your goals solely.

7. Social media is really an undervalued tool. Use social media as a source of motivation. To constantly create inspiration in your life, use your Facebook, Twitter, Instagram, or any other social media platform. Monitor and connect with people who have goals and plans like yours. Join with people who excel. Consult them in the areas where you want to achieve.

8. Build a support team of people who respect work and know what it takes to get a job. Surely you don't know what is needed to build a wall. You can say wow, fantastic, when you see a wonderful wall, but you don't know how to create one. Therefore, it is important to surround yourself with a knowledgeable team that knows what to do. Your team must have people in your profession on it and people with the same goals as yours. On the internet, there are lots of great, free classes. Check, track and observe what others are to achieve their objectives.

9. Do not compete with others. Maintain your own steady pace. If you want to be irritated, contrasting yourself with others is an effective way. It's going to kill your motivation. Even if you started

out happy, you will quickly lose your motivation if you begin to focus on what others have done. You should look at other people and watch their progress but never compare yourself to them. You have had experiences in life separate from them. You've got skills they haven't.

10. When you do not move on, it will slow down your development. Procrastination is your enemy; it's all right to take time to rest, but stalling will hurt your advancement every day. Leave your comfort zone and get inspired to do what you need to do.

11. Think about your mistakes without ruining your inspiration as you continue to focus on your previous mistakes. You can learn from past errors because you know now what to avoid. It's a new day. Engage yourself so what you want and deserve can be achieved.

12. Being self-motivated mean the right mindset - being clearly and intelligently open to constructive learning. It is all about positive thinking: a person who is optimistic foresees happiness, health, and prosperity and assumes that he or she can conquer any obstacle or challenge. You have to say you can do this, and it is feasible.

will happen. The only way you will find motivation is through positive thinking. Start even if you don't believe you are confident! Divert your attention. Motivation is workable, and you have the capacity to do it. You won't even have try to think positively.

13. Self-confidence: You need to think positively about yourself, not just about tasks or the universe. You must have faith in yourself and your skills.

Apparently self-love has many dimensions and there are a multitude of ways to sustain and develop it.

Chapter 12
Exercise and a Healthy Diet

Physical and mental wellness gets a lot of consideration these days. A sound body and strong mind can forestall unwanted conditions, for example, coronary illness and diabetes and assist you with keeping up as you age. There are great rewards of a more honed mind and body for a considerable length of time to come. Nothing helps self-love grow more than good health.

Mental wellness implies keeping your cerebrum and enthusiastic wellbeing fit as a fiddle. It doesn't mean preparing for the "mind Olympics" or acing an IQ test. It alludes to a progression of activities that will help you:

- slow down
- decompress
- boost a failing memory
- create a great mind-body association

The more you help your body, the more you help your psyche. Physical movement expands the progression of oxygen to the cerebrum. It additionally enhances the production of endorphins. It's not astonishing that individuals who are fit as a fiddle and will, in general, appreciate an elevated level of mental spryness.

Taking part in physical exercise will fighting depression and increase a positive point of view. It is the best way to beat life's pressures. Mental exercise is similarly advantageous. As indicated by in the Proceedings of the National Academy of Sciences, specific memory enhancing activities can build "liquid knowledge," or the capacity to reason and tackle new issues. While exercise is useful for the cerebrum and the body, so is reflection or contemplation. Quieting the brain, in meditation for example, permits you to tackle life's problems.

Advantages of mental wellness

At the point when you hit the hay in the wake of a monotonous day, your body starts to unwind. Yet, the brain doesn't generally follow. The part that controls thoughts and emotions is wide awake. How to quiet the mind? It can be full of idle thoughts, a bit of anger, dread or sorrow. We feel the bitterness and outrage that accompanies the passing of a friend or family member, a career misfortune or relationship issue, and other troublesome matters. Supporting our psychological well-being can stave off even the most negative feelings. It can even prevent the onset of a physical or psychological sickness. The three significant approaches to psychological wellness are: get physical, eat right, and assume responsibility for your stress.

Get Physical

We've known for quite a while the advantages of activity as a proactive method to improve our state of being and battle illness; presently, exercise a fundamental component in building and keeping mental wellness. Why?

- ♥ Physical action is a piece of the solution for the treatment of stress and tension. Exercise alone isn't a fix, yet it has a very positive effect.

- ♥ Research has discovered that regular physical action is as powerful as psychotherapy. Specialists report that patients who exercise consistently feel much improved and are less inclined to binge or misuse alcohol and medications.

- ♥ Exercise can decrease anxiety. Numerous studies have arrived at this resolution. Individuals who exercise report feeling less rushed or anxious. Indeed, even five minutes of a high-impact workout (a practice that requires oxygen, for example like swimming or jogging) can alleviate a great deal of stress.

- ♥ Physical exercise can neutralizing the emotional withdrawal, lethargy, and melancholy that characterize mental despondency. Studies show that both high-impact and anaerobic exercise (for example, weightlifting) have an impact.

- ♥ Moods and general well-being are entirely influenced by a good workout along with a boosted confidence and better overall body tone.

♥ Last but not least, exercise brings you into contact with others socially. For the length of exercise or yoga class, you can connect with individuals who share your enthusiasm for exercise.

Feel the Rush

We may not understand what caused it, yet a large portion of us have felt the rush. It is characteristic of intense exercise. Endorphin discharge increases like a revitalizing burst of energy after running for 10 minutes. Others will run for thirty minutes before this unexpected surge of energy kicks in. You don't need to over exercise to invigorate this endorphin discharge. It can happy in some times of therapy or certain medications, even during a vigorous massage. So appreciate even some moderate exercise and feel the endorphin rush!

Eat Right

Here's something worth mulling over – making good dietary decisions can influence more than our clothing size; it can affect our emotional wellness. A study by the UK's Mental Health Foundation recommends that an increasingly poor eating routine has negatively affected emotional wellness in recent years. Carbs and sugars ae the main culprits. In addition think of all the additives in processed food as well as the trans-fats that keep the cerebrum from working appropriately. Other studies make a powerful connection between changing nourishment trends and visible increments in Attention Deficit Hyperactivity Disorder, Alzheimer's, and schizophrenia.

The message is certainly not a new one, but it is the most compelling plea to give more consideration to the nutrition-psychological well-being association to enjoy self-love. What we put on our plates turns into crude material for our minds to produce hormones and impulse synapses that control our rest, state of mind, and conduct.

If we dupe the brain, we additionally scam our bodies. Our eating routines supply essential nutrients which our bodies need for mental and physical energy. Nutrient insufficiencies can cause mood swing and unsettling feels, long with a large group of physical issues.

Psychological well-being experts call attention to those tried and true dietary rules indispensable for individuals needing to treat weight gain, burgeoning bodily dysfunctions or mental behaviors. Choosing what to eat goes well beyond taste bud fulfillment. To enhance the work of the cerebrum, we have to eat a decent eating amount of:

- ♥ fresh leafy foods
- ♥ foods high in omega-3 unsaturated fats, for example, fish, nuts, seeds, and eggs

♥ protein

♥ whole grains

Chapter 13
Learn to Define What You Want

One of the biggest secrets to living a life filled with abundance and self-love is that we need to be specific. We need to ask the universe for what we want or it can't deliver us anything. By now, you would have seriously considered your belief system regarding your circumstances, financial situation, relationships, career, etc. have either worked for or against you. You may have had to change some of your thought processes quite drastically for these beliefs to be altered in any way.

The universe operates on a number of frequencies or vibrations that we cannot see or feel. We use these frequencies and vibrations to attract people and things into our lives. This is quite intense because once you understand how much power you have, you will find that your life can be changed quickly. When you hear the word "abundance", I am almost certain that the first thing that pops into your mind is money. Am I right? Well, that's not surprising at all because money is actually just another form of energy. This is where it gets really exciting in clearly defining what you want from the universe! If the universe operates on frequencies and vibrations, and money is just another form of energy, doesn't it stand to reason that if you can actually tap into this frequency or energy field, you can attract anything that you want?

We are so focused on the things we don't want that the universe is forced to deliver more and more of exactly the same. It is like a vicious cycle of stuff we don't want. The only way this cycle can be broken is when we do something about it. We need to physically step in and make a change. If you constantly focus on what you don't have, you will never have anything. If you focus on being lonely all the time, guess what? You are going to spend most of your time dealing with your own company.

We are going to look at identifying what you want and what you don't want and then project this back into the universe such that all your desires are fulfilled.

Be Clear About What You Don't Want

For the universe to give you everything you want, you need to make a conscious decision about all the things you don't want without really focusing on them. This can actually be hard because for the first time in your life, you will need to sit down and analyze your life for what it is right now. You need to face some harsh truths about your current reality (something that you create, by the way). Until you get to the point of saying to yourself that enough is enough and you either need or want to make some changes, nothing is going to happen.

I have already said that doubt or fear cannot exist in the same place as faith and belief. Unfortunately, negativity will almost always win, hands down, every time! It prevents us from progressing and moving forward, even if the movement is ever so slight. We must decide whether we are happy with the life we are currently living.

We spoke of the countless thought processes that go through your head daily? Well, this is part of the solution in being clear about what you don't want in your life anymore. Each of these thoughts needs to be followed through on some level. We can choose how we respond to the thoughts present in our brains. We can do this by practicing mindfulness techniques and becoming fully present in the moment, rather than living in the past or projecting ourselves into the future.

Some of these decisions are micro-decisions that you don't even need to think about because you have already been conditioned how to respond. An example of this would be switching off the hot tap if the water temperature is scalding; it's an automatic response. I'm talking about becoming more aware of the bigger decisions you face every day—almost all of these decisions are linked to our emotions or our feelings that the universe picks up. When we are feeling down, despondent and fearful, depressed and sad, guess what, this is exactly what the universe picks up and responds by delivering more of the same. With our freedom to choose, though, we can decide to focus on those things that will lift and elevate our mood to one of peace, joy, harmony, and happiness or even love.

These vibrations and energy levels are in keeping with the laws of the universe and ones it responds to better. Once you have made the choice about what you are no longer prepared to settle for in your life, it becomes easier to focus your energy on changing your thoughts and attracting those things you want instead.

Be Clear with Your Desires

Napoleon Hill gave the world one of the greatest pieces of advice about attracting abundance in his bestselling book, Think and Grow Rich (1937). It all starts with your freedom to choose what you would like from the universe. The one unique and divine gift we have all been blessed with is the power to choose exactly what we want. We have the power to choose how we feel, act, and how respond to certain situations. Every negative situation we experience can be altered into a positive one through the power of choice.

The most important thing when choosing what you want is to be as clear as possible. The universe cannot deliver on a vague request. If you decide that you want a new car, it doesn't help telling the universe that you just want a new car... it must it have leather seats and other luxurious features. If so, what luxury features would you like it to have? What color would you like it to be? How is it going to make you feel when you are sitting behind the wheel driving on the open road? Can you see the difference between the two messages that you send out into the universe? The first is vague and uninteresting, leaving a lot of room for interpretation and misunderstanding, while the second is accurate and detailed. The second version paints a clear picture of exactly what you would like. It gives the universe the vibration that you have already received and are currently experiencing joy. It produces a an emotion that the universe is able to work with. Once you have projected this request in a detailed manner, it suddenly becomes easier for it to manifest in your life.

The same is true of wishing you had more money. The universe doesn't know how much you would like—you must see the actual numbers, feel the emotions of how content you feel with complete financial freedom and how you can provide for your family. You need to feel all your negative emotions of the past disappearing as the chains of debt are broken. Are you wishing for a lump sum windfall like winning the lottery, or would you prefer a better source of financial security in the form of a better paying job? Possibly you want to create additional revenue streams that can supplement your current lifestyle. So what will these income streams look like, and how do you plan to manifest them? How will you feel once these wishes have been granted by the universe?

A word of caution: when you want the universe to grant you a financial wish… make sure you focus on wealth versus need. When you focus on needing more money, that is exactly what you are going to get. If you focus on getting out of debt, all the universe hears and understands is the word, "debt." You need to shift your focus on wealth and an abundance of money. When you do, that's what you will enjoy!

Of course, new cars and financial freedom are only some of the things you may desire from the universe, and they not the only things. These are materialistic comforts that make our lives more comfortable, sure, but there are many other things of value like love and stronger relationships, better careers, a comfortable home, loving families, and the freedom to travel to faraway places whenever you choose. You may also desire physical health and healing.

A reminder: self-love is self-knowledge and the ability to identify what to prioritize for yourself.

Chapter 14
Why do we Have to Put Ourselves First Before Everything Else?

Love yourself, before you love another

Self-love is a source of goodwill and respect. If these feelings are not enough, the relationship becomes authoritarian or is built on the duality of "victim - persecutor." Psychologists agree on one thing: self-love is essential to love other people too and generally feel comfortable.

First of all, it is good for your health. Self-love is the most reliable vaccine against all sorts of psychosomatic diseases and stress prevention. One who does not love himself first uses and then destroys the confidence of their partner. "The supplier of love" becomes embarrassed. He begins to doubt and eventually gets tired of proving his feelings. The mission is impossible: one cannot give to another that which he can give himself only - love of himself. One who does not love himself often unconsciously calls into question the feelings of another: so he's worse than me!" A lack of self-love can also take the form of an almost manic devotion, or obsession with love.

Understand that it is time to transform your attitude

Do you consider yourself a failure? Do you think there is nothing attractive in you to the opposite sex? All these thoughts are reflected not only on your face but also in your behavior, and in your daily communication with friends, colleagues, relatives. If a person in contact with others suffers, if he does not like his own life, then it is worth addressing. Is it worth changing yourself as hard as that might be. Can you learn to open yourself to the present and fall in love over again with yourself.

This understanding comes to different people in diverse ways; it is all hinges on the person. If he thinks about why he is not valued, respected or someone is constantly manipulating him, then these are visible signs of self-dislike. You may have to do something about it to stop suffering.

It is time to care for ourselves. A state of depression is when your own "I" is in the shadow of the "object" in a passive position. It happens when there is no faith in ourselves and we think that something good is only thanks to the efforts of other people, and not our own. Yes, heeding self-love means maintaining close and emotionally warm and stable love relationships, but that is not there is to it. Plus, a person who loves himself is not suffering from selfishness in wanting such relationships.

Learning to love yourself

How to go about caring yourself with all your supposed shortcomings?" We asked psychologists. And how practically and successfully should our love for ourselves be revealed? Assume that you are a mom and dad to yourself. Study how to love yourself from this position by discovering your requirements and desires, accepting mistakes as an experience, giving yourself support, and so on. But it is not likely that you can do it alone. Before getting professional help, start by saying, "I authorize support and will look after and cultivate myself." This is a positive can-do mindset.

Self-love techniques

Set objectives, even little ones, but be sure to attain them! Then applaud yourself and value your determination and efforts. Avoid popular slogans like "well done." Bear in mind that even the top business tycoons and celebrities are not without complexes. Take a piece of paper and split it into two columns or sides. List your strengths on the right and what you wish to alter in yourself on the left. If you attempt to be objective, you will see that there are more positive qualities in you than reasons for dissatisfaction with yourself and cultivating complexes.

Self-love should be promoted by caring for yourself in the arena of health and appearance. It is about complete self-satisfaction and not somebody else's desires. It is the necessary observance of what it takes to achieve self-love - both psychological and physical.

There are individuals for whom looking after kids, family, and other individuals comprises the meaning of life. How do they enjoy themselves more? It cannot always be in caring for other people while forgetting about themselves. When an individual makes caring for others a priority, as with children in their life, he is left without meaning. Excessive care does affirm one's value to a degree but it should not impair self-care.

How self-love differs from selfishness

Where does the border lie? Does self-love equate to common egoism? Psychologists have a lot to say here. Selfishness is totally determined by over valuing one's own advantages, putting ones interests above the well-being of others. A man who loves himself in the right way will never consider himself superior to others. He understands his value but also understands that everyone is as important as he is. Accordingly, he will treat others with respect and love.

Preferably, when an individual really loves himself, he generously provides it to others from the excess of love inside himself. And if one is selfish, then his love for himself will be selfish. Strictly speaking, it is more correct to talk not about love for oneself but about falling in love with oneself. Self-absorption and being charmed by the self entails an exaggeration of one's virtues, and such a love is quite selfish. If a person thinks about others and cares about them, then his love for himself is not connected with egoism in any way. Supplementing self-love with the attention and care for others is perhaps not difficult, but it is a completely separate kind of work.

It is easy and natural to love both oneself and others. Anyone who loves himself naturally does not devote too much time to it, just as a well-maintained garden does not require much trouble. It is easy to care for oneself to become a healthy and vigorous person. That is not a self-centered goal. It is the good side of self-love. The reality, however, is that those who become over preoccupied with self-love, at least initially become more selfish.

One of the mysteries of self-love is inner joy – the feeling of heat, light, and energy. But sometimes there is cold in your soul. If a person describes a picture of his inner world as dull and grey, like winter and maybe the lights have gone out, and there is no joy or energy and such a person lives without love. How to give birth and maintain light and warmth in your soul?

People often think that self-love consists of satisfying their simplest needs and pleasures, forgetting about their real-life duties and other people. Allow yourself to explore and do what you want, surround yourself with romance and give yourself gifts. There is no harm done, but the level of this love is not same as the love of a mother giving gifts to her child. Make no mistake about it. Recognizing the difference is part of developing true self-knowledge.

What are your real needs. They are not like those of a dependent child or even the desires and whims that spoiled children insist on getting. The essential thing is that they give joy in some form. With overindulgence, for the self or a child, everything becomes boring in the end, and the joy leaves. The same happens to an adult who deals in excess whether food, alcohol or shopping.

Satisfying needs in this way is not self-love. It doesn't always end with inner joy, light, and warmth. Such excesses are only a temporary measure and a substitute for self-love. This is a low-quality life, one that is not serious. Satisfying excessive needs is seen when a person seems to be buying luxuries because he does not love himself. If you really desire to move forward and develop, you need to care for other people, be needed, and master life with dignity and quality. You will have something to be proud of. If all needs come down to eating and entertain yourself with shopping or TV, then such a love of self is unlikely to be long-lasting.

Chapter 15

How the Lack of Love for Oneself Affects the People Around Us: Children, Husband, Friends?

Low self-esteem can degrade a child when either parent ignore him or her or fails to take notice of their achievements while harshly criticizing them for any mistakes made. The child feels there is no point in trying, and even if they do good, nothing will ever come out of it, so it is futile to excel.

Of course, it is not just the parents who develops this most unwelcome state. Families are always, and often wrongly, an easy target for culpability. It comes from anywhere, even teachers and peers. One of the worst crimes of all when I was a child was conceit.

On the contrary, parents don't want to instill conceit with too much praise. That is not self-esteem nor self-love. It promotes pride or envy. Scriptures tell us that pride and vanity are deadly sins, and the apparent reason is that we cannot love ourselves. We do not leave room for other people or things if we are full of pride and conceit.

On the other end of the coin, what if you are truly talented artist and always laden with praise. Will that engender conceit? Not if you, with a complete lack of self-esteem, turn around and say, "Well, that's kind of you, but it's not really very good." Some degree of self-love is valid and it doesn't have to tip the scales into conceit. Tooting your own horn is fine and accepting compliments is even better. The consequence of a lack of self-love is a lack of self-esteem. Here are the basic points of self-esteem.

- An honest appreciation of what we can do.
- Realizing our own values and abilities honestly.
- Being fully aware of our capabilities as well as shortcomings.
- Comprehension about our weaknesses.
- Not being too concerned about what other people might think of us.

Self-esteem means ignoring what others say, especially the negative. Your heart, mind, body, and spirit all need security and compassion. Therefore, in the cycle of healing from depression and reducing stress, self-love is so necessary.

Your spiritual development and recovery will be hindered without caring support and guidance, and a good amount self-love. Your nervous system needs security to unlock its trapped survival energy so you can enjoy life's pleasures with a cool, vigilant mind and stress-free body at last.

When you begin with some degree of self-love and self-acceptance, you are in a better place to allow someone else to support you in overcoming your pain. Here is an important truth when it comes to true inner healing: it takes a lot of courage because with emotional wounds, you will have to trust someone else.

If you have built strength and overcame the pain and tension in life, please applaud yourself right now. You are on the way to a lot of happiness and joy. You deserve a life free of fear and anxiety. Is it time to restore your nervous system because in many cases, you have been guilty of over-reacting or shutting down fully, and you do not want to function like this any longer. If so, just plan to respect yourself right now.

When looking in the mirror every morning when you brush your teeth, begin to increase your self-love by saying to yourself, "I esteem you." You can make the decision to stop criticizing yourself. I realize that this it is difficult to do. Harmful attitudes create negative feelings, which in the nervous system causes anxiety. Give yourself some freedom from bad conditioning, most definitely as a child and teenager, and learn new healthy habits of self-acceptance and self-love.

On the road to trauma healing and stress reduction, your self-love will accelerate your recovery and ensure the life full of joy and love that is your birthright. These feelings are supposed to go away while fear and anxiety are part of life and sometimes they get worse over time.

Anxiety disorders such as depression are among the most common mental illnesses in the US, and you can now, once and for all, resolve this epidemic with modern stress recovery methods. Trauma is no doubt a lifetime prison sentence. It is time to celebrate and encourage yourself to recover 100% from trauma. When you offer yourself the wonderful gift of self-love, your stress level will drop to a healthy level.

From Suicide to Self-love

Suicide is a permanent solution to a temporary problem. Nothing is worth taking a life for, particularly another man or woman. If someone has that much influence over you, do not have to continue with them in your life. Suck it up, walk away, take care of yourself and be the person you can be! Take the journey to self-love.

I was in that position once. I was sick from a divorce with all t typical gut-wrenching. I wanted to crawl in a hole and die in agony! It was nearly paralyzing at times. It was not until some years had gone by that I could take a step back and start to see more distinctly how I had played an enormous part in the split. I saw someone who did not take care of themselves the way they should have , and I took a good hard look at myself – a person with no to little self-love.

Yes, there was definitely a lack of self-love in my life at the time. Self-inflicted damage is not perceived as self-love! It was difficult to see anything lovable about myself through the haze of pain. But I knew I had to learn to love myself if I were ever to enjoy a healthy relationship. I would continue to draw unhealthy people into my existence if I remained psychologically sick. All I wanted to do was get smarter and more self-confident because a strong person is much more desirable than a weak person.

Love yourself, be true to yourself, and prioritize your well-being. Concentrate on a spiritual, physical, social, and intellectual focus on yourself. Set goals and carry them through at all times. Make positive comments to yourself. Surround yourself with people who are positive and uplifting. Do something good for yourself. For someone else, also do something nice. The list begins...

After all, if we cannot even recognize the good ourselves, how can we consider the good in someone else? When we cannot even re-spect ourselves, how can we expect others to respect us? In establishing a stable, loving relationship, self-love and self-acceptance are crucial first moves.

Note that love starts internally, and only when you achieve self-acceptance and self-love can you really express it with someone else. Anyone at the brink of suicide, or even entertaining suicidal thoughts, should know that there is light at the end of the tunnel.

Notes to attain more self-awareness:

Chapter 16

How to Improve Your Love Life by Starting to Love Yourself More?

Be firm but gracious when communicating your limits with others. Don't hide your self-love to give love. The key to expressing your boundaries or rebuffing a lover's premature sexual advances in an attractive way is to allude to your desire while also setting forth your standards.

Never be afraid to enforce your personal boundaries or express your limitations with a man. Doing so with poise and decorum will subconsciously communicate that you are a high-value woman, one with reasonable expectations. Women who can confidently tell a man what they want and do not want are rare and therefore VERY sought after.

Unfortunately, many women are terrified to set boundaries with a man they are highly attracted to because they fear he will lose interest, withdraw, or become completely turned off. These women believe that telling a man "no" or shutting down his premature sexual advances might drive away a potential boyfriend. If you struggle to set boundaries with men due to the deep fear of potential loss, you can stop worrying about it. Your fear of loss is groundless, and here is why: the men who will not be turned off by your limits are the ones who will cherish you the most.

Of course, if you are worried about coming across as "too demanding" or "not interested enough," try to use the "firm but enticing" technique. When you must express your limitations or outright reject a man's advances, simply state how you feel but use a hint of seduction to keep him intrigued. Here is a simple yet powerful step-by-step communication method for accomplishing this:

Communicate your boundaries and tell him, "no", in a clear but courteous way. Express why the boundary is important to you. You know it is about your self-love. For example, if a man is too sexually forward, it's one thing to tell him, "No, I'm not ready," and another thing to say, "Listen, Mike, I like you. A lot. I mean...you make me feel things I have never felt for any man before. But I am not ready for this yet. I want to give myself to the man who wants me for a lifetime. I hope you understand."

Did you see the difference there? The first boundary setting is perfectly fine, but it will not make his mind burn with anticipation and curiosity like the second one. And if "Mike" considers himself to be a potential "lifetime lover" candidate, he will do whatever he can to prove to you that he is the man for the job, no matter how long it takes.

By using the firm but the enticing technique, you will communicate your limits and make the right man desperate to see you again all at the same time. Men do not mind being rejected when done with grace and respect for their egos. A man is less likely to see your rejection as a sign of a "lack of interest" if you can communicate your boundaries with a sincere expression of desire.

Never make yourself a fool for flaky male behavior. You show no self-love by doing so. If you allow a man to flake on you once, he will most assuredly do it again...and again...and again. In the event that you are not familiar with the term, a "flake" is basically someone who does not follow through. They are major procrastinators, highly unreliable, and nearly incapable of keeping their word. In short, flakes make terrible friends and disastrous partners (both in love and in business) to those unfortunate enough to rely on them.

He becomes wishy-washy with his attention and might even break off contact with you as soon as you begin showing a serious interest in him. He disappears from time to time or does not respond in a reasonable amount of time when communicating with you and does not give a valid explanation for doing so. He cancels dates on short notice without suggesting a future date to make up for it or arrives unreasonably late with an attitude of indifference towards his tardiness. He defends his flakiness with the belief that he "doesn't owe you anything" and he can "do as he pleases," in spite of the fact you have already made a significant investment of love and loyalty in him.

Simply put, a man who flakes on you does not hold you in high regard. If he does not hold you in high regard, he does not deserve your attention. It does not really matter "why" he flaked, as men flake on women for a myriad of reasons that could spawn a book of its own (most of those reasons have nothing to do with you, by the way). Once you realize that a guy is not respectful of your time and attention, you must cease to entertain him and turn your attention to more persistent admirers. Rely on your self-love as it has good judgment!

Let us say a handsome gentleman (we will call him Mr. Handsome Face) you met through a friend of a friend has finally asked you out on a date. He tells you he is going to pick you up on Friday night at eight o'clock sharp. Excitedly, you prepare for the date well in advance with some long over-due personal beautification, and you even borrow a gorgeous outfit from one of your close friends (you know, the one who has ALL the clothes you like).

Friday evening arrives, and you eagerly wait for Mr. Handsome Face to show up. Seven-thirty rolls by, and you are almost done getting ready. Seven fifty rolls by, and you are done up properly and waiting patiently on your couch, trying to read a novel to distract yourself. Eight o'clock rolls by, and you are expecting him to knock on your door at any moment. Eight fifteen rolls by, and naturally, you are getting a little over-anxious. Eight-thirty rolls by, and now you are getting a little concerned. Do you ignore his tardiness and go on the date anyway. Do you graciously ask for an explanation and then politely refuse the date if he does not have one.

Maybe you decide to throw a drink in his face right before you slam the door on him. As a self-possessed woman of class, I'm going to assume you wanted to communicate that your attention is valuable and your good graces are not cheap commodities. Accepting a man's extreme tardiness without a reasonable excuse goes beyond being are "easy-going". He'll simply think you're "easy." Not having standards or setting boundaries when it comes to your attention forces a man to make a value judgment about you that tells him: she is not worth my best wooing efforts. Don't defy your self-love.

Let's be real here. Being unreasonably late or doing something that is basically bad manners is not the kind of behavior anyone should encourage. If you consistently entertain such behavior you, will find that people will not respect your time, which ultimately means that they do not respect you. If you begin making allowances for such a guy early on without some sort of polite penalty or gracious reprimand, he will not value the attention you give him and thus, he will not respect you. And if you do not know it by now, a man will not commit his all to a woman if he does not respect her.

Do not tolerate men who show indifference towards your tender display of emotions and violate your self-love. Use your emotional vulnerabilities to test a man's compassion, esteem, and earnestness of affection for you. Only the man with a kindred soul will be drawn to you, even more, when you share your soul with him.

One of the most effective things you can do to determine if a man is genuinely interested is to share your vulnerable, then observe how he responds (assuming he responds at all). Of course, you do not have to confess your deepest darkest secrets, but instead, share private little intimacies that you would not share with the average person.

Such private merriments may include but are not limited to cherished childhood memories, painful memories from your past, such as a friend's betrayal, present-day struggles, such as your fear of switching careers or the issues you are having with a co-worker. Add some quirky interests you are passionate (or obsessed) about, things that make you deeply emotional, such as mistreated pets, domestic violence, your church's ministry, or your sister's rehab journey.

If you open up about such things and Mr. Tall-Dark-and-Hand-some does not appear even remotely interested, moved, or engaged with what you're saying, he's probably not as into you as you had hoped. When a man has a sincere, romantic interest in a woman, he will not hide his sympathies and enthusiasm whenever she shares the beautiful varieties of her emotions with him.

The truth is, getting emotional with the man you are dating will either frighten him away (Mr. Wrong) or draw him closer to you (Mr. Right), so you cannot lose with this strategy. Becoming vulnerable with a guy allows him to catch glimpses of your soul. And if he is Mr. Right, he will become even more curious and infatuated with you over time. He will see you as a "kindred soul," so to speak, and will feel even more emotionally drawn to you in the process.

Now, my only caveat with this approach is to be sure that you are only showing glimpses into your soul. Things can easily backfire if you spew out the contents of your heart all in one go. Doing so can potentially frighten guys away if you are not discerning. You want to reveal just enough of your heart to see if he can engage with you on an emotional level, but not so much that he feels overwhelmed all at once.

Chapter 17

Narcissism and Self-love

There is more to narcissism than having an inflated sense of self and being conceited and egotistical. It is by no means the definition of self-love. Yes, these are all unattractive qualities when in the extreme; however, true narcissism involves a maniacal pursuit of praise, ambition, and gratification. Those who suffer from the slightest degree of NPD can be arrogant, smug, and vain and have an unusually high level of self-esteem. This is their outward appearance, but deep down, they are extremely insecure and feel as if they have little self-worth – the opposite of self-love. They thrive off admiration from others, which is how they feed their belief that they are more important than anyone else.

Psychologists refer to this as "narcissistic supply," and it is almost like a drug for the narcissist. They are addicted to receiving confirmation that they are indeed superior beings. Typically, narcissists do not have an empathetic bone in their body, which basically means that they do not have a care in the world for anyone apart from themselves.

There are different degrees of narcissism; in fact, psychologists believe that we are all slightly narcissistic. It is even possible that narcissism is required as a method of survival in the world today. Being a little egotistical can be beneficial; however, the behavior of a fully narcissistic individual is very destructive if it surpasses the normal boundaries of self-love.

To be considered narcissistic, their behavior reflects the following:

- They blow situations out of proportion and are incapable of putting things into perspective.

- They are unable to empathize with the feelings or thoughts of others.

- They are only concerned with their own issues.

- They have no respect for authority.

- Deep down, they feels inferior and will compensate by doing everything they can to be seen as superior.

- They are incapable of receiving constructive criticism.

- They need sexual admiration and are often exhibitionists.

- They are vain, exploitative, and dependent on others.

To a certain degree, all people who have been diagnosed with NPD exhibit these traits. However, there are other types of narcissistic behaviors that therapists divide into several categories.

Narcissism in children is typically the result of learned behavior from their primary caregivers and can be unlearned. Therefore, psychologists are reluctant to diagnose children with NPD. Fully-fledged NPD only exists in adults and is treated differently; other types of narcissism include the following.

Phallic narcissists are typically males who have a great love for themselves and their physical bodies (not a good form of self-love). They strut like roosters and are very aggressive and athletic. They are exhibitionists who enjoy putting their bodies on display.

The manipulative narcissist: They enjoy manipulating and influencing others. The manipulative narcissist feeds their need for power by manipulating, bullying, lying, and intimidating others.

The paranoid narcissist: The paranoid narcissist suffers from a deep self-hatred; they project this onto others with extreme jealous behavior, and they are overly sensitive to criticism.

The craving narcissist: Although narcissists are extremely egotistical, craving narcissists are very needy, demanding of love, emotionally clingy, and attention-seeking.

The most significant personality trait of a narcissist is grandiosity. If a person does not stop going on about how they were the MVP of their college basketball team at a dinner party, it might show that that individual is boastful, conceited, or even a little ill-mannered. This can be extremely annoying; however, it is not narcissistic if it is true. But if the person did not even play on the team but sat on the bench all season, that is being grandiose.

What Causes Narcissism?

Babies are born selfish—it is natural. Their number one concern is getting their immediate needs met, and that is it. It is self-love that runs amok. They have zero understanding of other people's desires and needs. To care for and protect themselves, children need to develop a healthy level of self-esteem, while at the same time caring about others to stay connected to society and family and avoid dangerous influences.

When a child has a healthy level of self-esteem, it is an indication that a child feels that they are worthy and loved within their family and valuable to society. The essence of a healthy self-esteem is not feelings of self-centeredness because the individual does not feel as if they need to trample on others to get their needs met.

There must be a transformation in childish self-centered behavior in order to experience sound mental health in adulthood and attain true self-love. The ability to function effectively in a family and in society is dependent upon the child's ability to gradually see other people's points of view and to experience empathy. So, an emotionally healthy child should eventually become sincere about the well-being of others. The inability to develop empathy as a child is a red flag that they may be at risk of developing a personality disorder in adulthood like narcissism.

Preteens do not have the mental capability to be manipulative, which is why mental health professionals are reluctant to diagnose NPD any earlier than the age of 18. However, there are certain behaviors in teenagers that indicate that the possibility of developing the condition in adulthood.

- Continuous bullying behaviors such as degrading, threatening, making fun of, or scapegoating people, including their parents and other adults

- The desire to win regardless of who gets hurt

- Constant lying, even lying about the lies they tell, blaming others for their lies, and refusing to accept accountability by attacking those who report them to their parents

- A high and unnatural sense of self-worth

- Determined to get their needs met over others

- An attitude of extreme entitlement leads them to act as if they should be treated differently than anyone else and that regardless of the circumstances, they should get what they want

- Aggressive responses to being wronged, criticized, or upset

- Constantly blaming others when things do not work out the way they want

- Less cooperative and more competitive

The bottom line is that NPD is the result of the family environment a child was raised in. All children want the attention and approval of their parents, and they adapt to their surroundings the best they can. It is a hard road to self-love at times. However, there are some home environments so destructive that the only way a child is capable of adapting is to become narcissistic.

Unconditional Versus Conditional Love – The Effects

Everyone wants to be loved unconditionally for who they are. If children feel that their parents only love and value them because they are special, this can lead to insecurity and destroy self-love. It is impossible to win all the time, and there is always going to be someone else out there who is better than you in some way. Children whose parents idealize them end up believing they are only worthy when they are being idealized. If not, they feel as if they have failed at life.

Children who are idealized become ashamed when they realize that they are not the perfect people their parents raised them to be. They cannot handle the fact that they have flaws like everyone else and so strive to be perfect in every area of their lives.

They are unable to identify who they really are. They only focus on doing the things that will appease their parents and win their approval. They never spend time exploring their true identity and discovering what their interests are and where their talents lie.

Occasionally, the golden child may resist their prescribed role and avoid becoming narcissistic. They actually feel embarrassed by the over-the-top praise they receive. They don't want a false sense of self-love. The role that has been ascribed to them becomes somewhat of a burden. For example, one child of an excessive overbearing parent told his mother that he no longer wished to be a part of the family circus and would like to live his life without having to live up to the expectations of his overachieving parents.

The Exhibitionist Admirer

The exhibitionist narcissist parent will reward their children with attention and praise as long as they remain subservient to and admire the parent. These children are trained how to be narcissistic, but at the same time, they are prohibited from being in the limelight. The role they play within the family is to worship the awesomeness of the narcissistic parent without ever being critical of them or trying to surpass them in greatness.

This is how closet or covert narcissists come about; the children learn to be provided with the narcissistic supplies of praise and attention if they refrain from competing with their narcissistic parents. If they ever attempt to openly acknowledge that they are special, these supplies are withheld. The value they are given is based on their ability to act as a crutch to the egotistical nature of the exhibitionist parent.

As adults, children raised in these families feel too vulnerable, exposed, and uncomfortable to be in the spotlight, so their self-esteem and narcissism issues are not as obvious not close to them. No one really knows that they have taken a big hit to their self-love. Some take on the role and play it very well, ending up in a job supporting an overachieving exhibitionist narcissist that they have nothing but admiration for.

The Bottom Line

If you are ever concerned that the person you have met may have narcissistic tendencies, ask about their childhood and what their parents were like. Once you get a clear picture of their home environment, it will not be difficult to work out whether they have narcissistic tendencies or not. It is hard to engage in a relationship with a narcissist who does not have self-love.

Chapter 18
The Nature of Emotions

Your negative emotions are not bad or useless.

You may blame yourself for experiencing negative emotions, or, perhaps, you see yourself as mentally weak. However, despite what your inner voice might say, your emotions are not bad. Emotions are simply emotions. Nothing more.

As such, being depressed does not make you less of a person than you were three weeks ago when you were happy. Feeling sad now does not mean you will never be able to laugh again. Remember this: the way you interpret emotions, as well as the blame game you engage in, creates suffering, not the emotions themselves.

The fleeting nature of emotions

No matter how depressed you are, how much grief you are experiencing, or how horrible you feel at a given point in time, this shall pass. Look at some of the negative emotions you experienced in the past. Remember the worst times in your life. During these most difficult periods, you were probably so caught up in your emotions that you imagined never being able to escape them. You could not imagine being happy again. But even these episodes ended. Eventually, the clouds dissipated, and the real you shone once again.

Your emotions come and they go. Your depression will go, your sadness will vanish, and your anger will fade away. Bear in mind, if you experience the same emotions repeatedly, it probably means you hold disempowering beliefs and need to change something in your life. If you suffer from severe, chronic depression, it might be a good idea to consult a specialist.

The trickiness of emotions

Have you ever felt that you will never be happy again? Have you ever been so attached to your emotions you thought they would never go away? Do not worry, and it is a common feeling. Negative emotions act as a filter that taints the quality of your experiences. During a negative episode, every experience is perceived through this filter. While the world outside may remain the same, you will experience it in a completely different way .

For instance, when you are depressed, you do not enjoy the food you eat, the movies you see, or the activities in which you engage. You only see the negative side of things, feeling trapped and powerless. On the other hand, when you are in a positive mood, everything in life appears better. Food tastes great, you are naturally friendlier, and you enjoy all the activities you partake in.

You may now believe that armed with the knowledge you have gained from this book, you will never be depressed again. Wrong! You will keep experiencing sadness, frustration, depression, or resentment, but hopefully, each time these occur, you will become wiser and wiser, remembering that this, too, shall pass.

I have to admit that I can easily be fooled by my emotions. While I know I am not my emotions, I still give them too much credit and fail to realize they are just temporary visitors. More importantly, I fail to remember they are not me. Emotions always come and go, but I remain. Once the emotional storm has passed, I generally feel like an idiot for having taken my emotions so seriously. Do you?

Interestingly, external factors might not be—and often are not—the direct cause of a sudden change in your emotional state. You can be in the exact same situation, with the same job, the same amount of money in your bank account, and have the same problems as always, but experience radically different emotional states. In fact, if you look at your past, you will see that this is often what happens. You are mildly depressed for a couple of hours or a few days before bouncing back to your "default" emotional state. During this period of emotional stress, your environment does not change at all. The only thing that changes is your internal dialogue.

Negative emotions are like a spell. While you are under their influence, breaking free seems impossible. You may know that dwelling on the same thoughts is pointless, yet you cannot help but go with the flow. Feeling an intense pull, you keep identifying with your thoughts and, as a result, feel worse and worse. When this happens, no rational argument seems to work. The more these emotions fit your personal story, the stronger the pull becomes.

The filtering power of emotions

Your emotional state can drastically affect your outlook on life, leading you to act and behave differently. When you are in a good state, you have more energy available. This gives you:

- More confidence in everything you do

- The openness to consider new actions that could improve your life

- The ability to leave or break out of your comfort zone

- More emotional room to persevere during tough times

- Better ideas and enhanced creativity, and

- Easy access to positive emotions within the same emotional range.

When you are in a negative state of mind, you have less energy available, giving you:

- A lack of confidence that affects everything you do

- A lack of motivation that reduces the scope of actions you are willing to take

- A reluctance to take on new challenges and leave your comfort zone

- A reduced ability to persevere in the face of setbacks, and

- A propensity to attract negative thoughts within the same emotional range.

Let us have a look at a real-life example from my own life. Both cases happened under the same external conditions. The only difference was my emotional state at the time.

Case 1 - feeling excited about my online business led to these thoughts and actions:

- An openness to consider new courses of action: I am open to new ideas or to work on a new project. I can think of ways to collaborate with other authors and start building a new coaching program to offer my audience.

- The ability to get out of my comfort zone: It becomes easier for me to push myself beyond my comfort zone. I may contact people I don't know or run Facebook Lives, for instance.

- More emotional room to persevere I stick to my projects even when I lack motivation.

- Better ideas and enhanced creativity. I am open to new ideas. I might come up with new ideas for books, articles, or other creative projects.

- Easy access to more positive emotions: I attract more positive emotions. At the same time, my mind rejects negative thoughts more easily by refusing to identify with them.

Case 2 - Feeling mildly depressed due to my lack of results:

- A lack of confidence: I start doubting myself and all the projects I am currently working on. Suddenly, everything I do becomes useless or "not good enough". Thoughts like, "What's the point?", "I'm not going to make it," or "I'm stupid," cross my mind. Needless to say, promoting myself becomes a major challenge.

- A lack of motivation: I do not feel like doing anything. I am attacked by and am unable to escape negative thoughts. I have the same negative thoughts again and again, which repeat like a broken record. They seem so real and taint all my experiences.

- A difficulty to take on new challenges: I have little energy left over to leave my comfort and undertake challenging projects.

Chapter 19
How to Build Self-Confidence

If you want to be seen as confident and reap the benefits that come with self-confidence, make sure you walk the walk that goes along with the talk. This means you need to start building the traits of a self-confident individual. As you develop these traits, you will find that you are far more likely to succeed in your interactions with other people. People tend to love those who are self-confident, and if you can manage to make yourself as self-confident as you reasonably can, you will find that your own positivity will attract more positivity into your life.

Believing in Yourself

Perhaps the most important step in becoming self-confident is beginning to believe in yourself. This is a tough one, as most people find that they struggle, at least in some capacity, with believing in themselves from time to time. Do not worry—you do not have to believe in yourself all of the time. In fact, you should absolutely know how to tell what your weaknesses are as they arise, allowing you to tell whether you are actually capable of doing something or not.

Remember, a major portion of being self-confident is knowing your own abilities, good and bad. Even knowing your weaknesses and having a realistic idea of when it is best to completely reject the idea of doing something can be considered self-confident. This does not mean you lack self-confidence; in fact, it solidifies the self-confidence you do have because you recognize that your inability would prevent you from safely completing the request.

When you can do whatever is being requested, it is important that you believe in yourself. It is okay to be afraid of failing, but actually allowing yourself to fail due to inaction is far worse. If you feel you are entirely incapable of everything, then start branching out. Trust yourself enough to learn. Respect yourself enough to give it a legitimate try. Love yourself enough not to quit needlessly when you could have legitimately finished the project with a bit of extra effort.

The bird trusted itself when it leapt from the nest for the first time trying to fly. The baby trusted himself enough to let go of the edge of the sofa he was holding onto while trying to walk. You can push yourself over the edge and do things, too. Just believe that you can and give it your best shot. The worst that could happen is a failure, and failing is rarely as bad as people think it will be.

Persuading Yourself

When you find that you cannot believe in yourself for some reason, it is time to persuade yourself to do so. Your self-confidence is based on your own self-reflection and your ability to acknowledge your strengths and weaknesses. You need to be willing to convince yourself that what you are asking of yourself is not something impossible. It is not something that is even scary—all you need to do is give it a shot, and if you fail, you just try again.

This can be a scary one for many people—it is tough trying to look at yourself as someone capable after a lifetime of self-doubt. However, life on the other side is much more pleasant. Instead of being afraid of failing and letting that fear cripple and stunt you, you are using it as a launching pad. Everything was new to you at some point, and that is okay. Everything was new to everyone at some point—even the people next to you to whom you are comparing yourself were new at something. They started this life with exactly what you did: a blank slate. It is up to you what you do with that blank slate.

When you are trying to convince yourself to try something or feel a bit more confident, stop and think about what you are good at. Everyone is good at something—you just need to figure out what that is for you. If you cannot think of something you are good at, try some new things. Find a few new hobbies, something you can take pride in. That pride will boost your self-confidence that will permeate other aspects of your life.

When you do find those things you are good at, latch onto them. Remind yourself that you have permission not to be good at everything you attempt but you are also skilled at several different things, such as your ability to engage in whatever that newfound hobby is.

If you still fail to come up with anything you are good at, try asking the people you trust. If you were to go up to a loved one or a trusted friend and say that you are working on your self-confidence but really struggling to identify something you are good at, you will probably get a few suggestions. You may find that you are significantly better at plenty of things and some you never really expected; and that alone can boost up some confidence.

Letting Go of Negative Thoughts

Negative thoughts tend to be at the root of all our struggles with self-confidence. If you struggle to be self-confident, it is probably because you have all sorts of negative thoughts swirling around in your mind, and they can be dangerous if you let them continue to grow unchecked. When they grow and fester, more and more of your thinking and ability to accept your own abilities will become negative as well. Negativity is contagious, after all.

Think about the last time you bought berries and left them in your fridge for too long. One berry begins to mold and soon that mold spreads and takes over all the berries nearby, even though several of those berries may have been perfectly ripe. Your negativity is like the mold on the berry—it will spread. It will begin to infect other areas of your life. Your one negative thought can slowly become two, then three, and eventually a negative thought process will become your natural state of being. You must stop trying to avoid negativity and instead unintentionally embrace it. In embracing negativity, you will discover the dangers of negativity, and any confidence you may have had will pay for it.

Ignoring Other People's Opinions

When you lack self-confidence, much of your life is spent worrying and wondering how other people feel about you. Instead of focusing on how you feel in your skin, you start to put value in the feelings of other people. Make sure you are taking the road that most people would agree is best. Stop thinking about what you want or who you want to be and instead begin to focus on becoming who you want to be.

Remember, the only person whose opinions matter is yourself. Ultimately, if no one else likes who you are or what you choose to do with yourself, that is their own loss. You do not need to live your life trying to prove yourself to other people. You need to assign your own self-worth and look at it through your own eyes. When you are willing to ignore the opinions of others, you learn to be truer to yourself. You learn to embrace what you love, no matter the consequence. You no longer see situations as ways to be embarrassed. An accident is no longer a mortifying event. All that matters is how you are feeling about yourself because, ultimately, the only one who has to live with you is yourself.

Focusing on Positivity

Finally, when you want to build self-confidence, you need to not only leave behind the negativity but also focus on positivity. Stop worrying about what went wrong—accidents happen. People are not perfect. Not everything is going to work out according to plan. However, you should be capable of dealing with the instances in which things do not go as expected. This means that you should be capable of recognizing positivity when you see it.

There is almost always something positive to be found, even in the worst of situations. For example, is a car accident that kills someone who becomes an organ donor and saves five other lives really all bad? Yes, the fact that the one person died is terrible, but there are five positives right there as well. That does not mean you cannot grieve if someone dies or be upset about something going wrong. However, instead of letting that grief or upset consume you, try to find the positives. Do not cry that you lost someone—be glad that you had them to begin with.

Conclusion

It's natural for people to criticize themselves. The imperfections or mistakes that we let our inner critic beat us up over are often not even noticed by the people around us. The funny thing is that we do this mostly because we hold ourselves to a higher standard than other people.

When you let yourself feel that you are not good enough, you get stuck in a cycle of negative thinking and self-hatred. This could eventually lead to you develop what we refer to as your negative inner voice. That voice inside your head keeps putting you down and reminding you of all your mistakes and all the things that are ugly about you.

If you continue to listen to your negative inner voice, you might start to believe it when it tells you that you are stupid or embarrassing. It will continue to go unchecked as you stop challenging these dangerous ideas that come across your mind. You could start to feel helpless and start to believe that this is the way life is or the way things are, and that there is no way to change these "truths" about yourself.

Your self-esteem and confidence then take a blow, and you may begin to withdraw yourself from people. In some cases, instead of withdrawing, you might instead take the opposite approach and start to present your outer self as superior to other people. You are doing this for the simple fact that you want to be accepted, but most of the time, it may just cause people to dislike or resent you. This happened to me. I started to project an image that I was cool and ended up alienating people. It is almost second nature for people to present themselves in the best light possible, even as children. We learn from an early age that people-pleasing gets us special attention, gifts, and unique privileges. As a result, we learn that this is what relationships with other people are built on, when in fact, it is just an interaction.

If we continue to be people-pleasers because of a desire to be liked and avoid criticism, we carry these same patterns into adulthood, and we continue to listen to the negative inner voice that is leading us along the way. When you do not have a high view of yourself, you are likely not to take in those moments where people are praising you. It feels uncomfortable because you do not feel like you deserve these compliments, even when you know deep down that you did something worthy of the praise. You might not know how to handle these compliments because they cause friction with how you feel about yourself on the inside.

On the other hand, when someone criticizes you, this feels more comfortable as it is how you feel inwardly. It feels more natural because the negativity might be ingrained in you. You are likely used to having negative dialogue run through your mind more often than not. It is certainly a red flag if you are able to accept criticism better than you do a compliment.

We hope this book about self-love was helpful, and we wish you all love and happiness in your daily lives!

www.ingramcontent.com/pod-product-compliance
Lightning Source LLC
Chambersburg PA
CBHW070744030726
47601CB00001B/137